Vital Records

of the

First Independent (now Unitarian) Church

Baltimore, Maryland 1818-1921

Edited and arranged by
Mrs. Edwin C. Gibbons, Jr.

HERITAGE BOOKS
2007

HERITAGE BOOKS
AN IMPRINT OF HERITAGE BOOKS, INC.

Books, CDs, and more—Worldwide

For our listing of thousands of titles see our website
at
www.HeritageBooks.com

Published 2007 by
HERITAGE BOOKS, INC.
Publishing Division
65 East Main Street
Westminster, Maryland 21157-5026

International Standard Book Number: 978-1-58549-507-8

FOREWORD

THE CHURCH

Unitarianism, a movement which in the United States first arose in New England in the closing years of the eighteenth century, was introduced into Maryland by the Rev. James Freeman, pastor of King's Chapel, Boston, who upon invitation delivered a series of lectures in Baltimore in 1816. His audiences were described as "large and resepectable," and upon his departure many of those who had heard him speak continued to gather weekly for further discussions in private homes. At a meeting on February 10, 1817, it was decided to set about the estblishment of a Unitarian Church in the City of Baltimore, and a nine-member board of trustees was chosen for the purpose from among those favorable to the work.

The site selected by the trustees for the church building was at the corner of what are today North Charles and West Franklin Streets, and the architect they engaged was Maximilien Godefroy. The structure arose on schedule, and on October 29, 1818 it was dedicated as the First Independent Church.

On May 5, 1819, the "Baltimore Sermon," a controversial presentation of the main points of Unitarianism, was delivered in the church by the visiting Rev. William Ellery Channing of Boston, but it was a younger New Englander, the Rev. Jared Sparks, who served from 1819 to 1823 as the Baltimore congregation's first minister. Sparks later went on to a distinguished scholarly career and to accept the ultimate New England honor, the presidency of Harvard.

Many prominent nineteenth-century Baltimoreans had New England roots, and most who did tended to gravitate towards churches which could make the same claim. Enoch Pratt, the celebrated philanthropist, was born in North Middleborough, Massachusetts, in 1808, but died an active member of the Baltimore Unitarian congregation in 1896. Almost an equal number of Baltimore Unitarians, however, were Maryland natives or immigrants to the city from places further south, and with the approach of the Civil War some of these began to detect an unpleasant "Yankee" tinge to the First Independent Church. In 1858, a group of these dissidents broke away to form a Second Independent Church, which endured in various locations around the city for fourteen years. In 1872 the Second Church was dissolved, and most of its members re-joined the First Church.

In 1935 the Universalist Church of Baltimore, which had been established in 1831, merged with the First Independent Church, and the resulting congregation assumed the name it still bears today, First Unitarian Church (Unitarian and Universalist). It continues in operation at its historic West Franklin Street location.

FOREWORD

THE GRAVEYARD

Between 1820 and 1824, the First Independent Church purchased a 1 1/2-acre lot at the place in East Baltimore where North Gay Street crossed the northern end of Broadway. The tract was divided into 278 plots, which were offered for sale as burial places for between $15 and $30 each.

The cemetery was not a financial success; less than half the lots were ever sold, and there were few burials in those that were. In 1872, anxious to rid itself of the financial obligation the upkeep of the graveyard entailed, the church membership voted to close the cemetery, exhume and relocate the bodies it contained, and sell the property. In May, 1872, the bodies of 32 adults and 16 children were exhumed. Those not claimed by relatives were moved to Lots 289 and 290 in Area EE of nearby Baltimore Cemetery.

The graveyard lot was sold to Enoch Pratt, a trustee of the First Independent Church. In 1876, part of it was condemned by the city for the northward extension of Broadway; the rest was developed for house lots by Mr. Pratt.

THE RECORDS

The Maryland Historical Society possesses a photostatic copy of the earliest record book of the First Independent Church, and it is from this photostatic copy – made in 1929 – that the information contained in this volume is taken. It covers records kept by the following Unitarian ministers:

Rev. Jared Sparks (1819-1823)
Rev. George W. Burnap (1827-1859)
Rev. Nathan H. Chamberlain (1860-1863)
Rev. John F.W. Ware (1864-1867)
Rev. Edward C. Guild (1868-1871)
Rev. Charles R. Weld (1872-1898)
Rev. William B. Geohegan (1900-1901)
Rev. Alfred B. Hussey (1902-1916)
Rev. Charles A. Wing (1917-1919)
Rev. Harry F. Burns (1921)

The contents of this book are basically verbatim transcripts of the entries in the Historical Society's photostat of the original records. The editor, Mrs. Edwin C. Gibbons, Jr., has done extensive work with contemporary census records in order to decipher illegible names and verify questionable dates. The original records remain in the possession of the First Unitarian Church.

Francis O'Neill

ABBREVIATIONS

b.....................................born

bapt..................................baptized

comm..................................communicant

conf..................................confirmed

d.....................................died

dau...................................daughter

hus...................................husband

m.....................................married

p.....................................parents

PIONEER MINISTERS

1819 – 1823	Jared Sparks – first minister of the First Independent church of Baltimore at Charles and Franklin Streets, Baltimore; later became president of Harvard University; cornerstone of church laid 6/5/1817
1827 – 1859	George Washington Burnap
1860 – 1863	Nathan Henry Chamberlain
1864 – 1867	John Fothergill Waterhouse Ware
1868 – 1871	Edward Chipman Guild
1872 – 1898	Charles Richmond Weld
1900 – 1901	William B. Geohegan
1902 – 1916	Alfred Rodman Hussey

ABRAHAM Alice m Mar 21 1894 to Frederick A.L. Schluter, both of Baltimore
    p 131
ALLEN Allston m Elizabeth, father of Julia Minard p 29, Harriet p 29, Mary
    Ordway p 29, Frank Allston p 29, Catherine Tracy p 41, Eleanor Easter p 41
ALLEN Catherine Tracy b Jul 8 1847, dau of Allston and Elizabeth Allen, bapt
    in Jersey City NJ Jul 30 1854 p 41
ALLEN Eleanor Easter b Jan 17 1850, bapt in Jersey City NJ Jul 30 1854, dau
    of Allston and Elizabeth Allen p 41
ALLEN Frank Allston b 1843, bapt May 30 1844, son of Allston and Elizabeth
    Allen p 29
ALLEN Hannah E. m to Luther W. Mason Oct 16 1845 p 111
ALLEN Harriet b Aug 18 1838, bapt May 30 1844, dau of Allston and Elizabeth
    Allen p 29
ALLEN Julia Minard b Feb 6 1836, bapt May 30 1844, dau of Allston and
    Elizabeth Allen p 29
ALLEN Mary Ordway b Oct 24 1840, bapt May 30 1844, dau of Allston and
    Elizabeth p 29
ANGLAR Calvin bapt Oct 12 1837 p 16
APPLETON Caroline Havers bapt Jun 1 1822, dau of   and William G.
    Appleton p 8
APPLETON Charles H. hus of Hannah, father of George Dawes p 2, Mary Dawes
    p 5, Thomas Dawes p 8, Charlotte Dawes p 12, Henry Dawes p 14, Edward
    Dawes p 14
APPLETON Charlotte Dawes dau of Charles H. and Hannah Appleton, bapt Jul 1
    1824, m to John Cranch(?) Apr 15 1845 pp 12 and 110
APPLETON Edward Dawes son of Charles H. and Hannah Appleton, bapt Jun 4
    1828 p 14
APPLETON George Dawes son of Charles H. and Hannah Appleton, b Oct 6 1818
    in Baltimore County, bapt Nov 8 1818 p 2
APPLETON Henry Dawes son of Charles H. and Hannah Appleton, bapt Jun 4 1828
    p 14
APPLETON Margaret Dawes m Russell Sturgis Dec 19 1835 p 107
APPLETON Mary Dawes dau of Charles H. and Hannah, bapt Nov 19 1820 p 5
APPLETON Thomas Dawes son of Charles H. and Hannah Appleton, bapt Jun 10
    1822 p 8
ARCHER Caroline m Leonard J. Wyeth Oct 2 1821 p 102
ARNOLD Henry N. of New York NY, m Sophia Plum(?) of Reno NV Feb 21 1912 p 136
ATCHESON Mary m to Henry MacHale(?) Jun 28 1855 p 115
ATWELL Richard Henry m to Caroline Augusta Cengle Apr 15 1841 p 109
ATWILL R.A. listed as a comm of the church after 1865 and prior to 1869 p 78
AYRES Emily D. m to Captain Rezin G. Howell at the U.S. Barracks, Washington
    DC on Feb 6 1884, second dau of Major General Ayres, USA p 127
AYRES General father of Emily D. p 127, Mary Bartlett p 126, headquartered
    at the U.S. Barracks, Washington DC p 126
AYRES Mary Bartlett m to Lieut Edward E. Gayle on Mar 9 1881 at the U.S.
    Barracks, Washington DC p 126
BAILEY Mary E. m to Benjamin F. Bowles on Oct 22 1857 p 116
BAIRD Sophronia M. m to Edmund F. Wiswale(?) on Dec 4 1856 p 116
BAKER Ida Belle conf on Good Friday Apr 12 1895, joined church on Easter
    Sunday Apr 14 1895 p 87
BALDWIN Anna Lee conf on Whitsunday May 19 1907 by Alfred Rodman Hussey p 91
BALDWIN Cidney m to Moses S. Carpenter on Sep 27 1855 p 115

BALL Frank Webster of Grand Rapids MI m to Josephine Griswold Lungrew of
    Toledo OH on Feb 22 1877 p 126
BANNING Charles Henry son of Joseph and Rebecca Banning, b Jun 7 1844, bapt
    Dec 22 1846 p 32
BANNING Joseph hus of Rebecca, father of Charles Henry p 32
BARGET Elizabeth conf on Whitsunday May 30 1909 by Alfred Rodman Hussey p 92
BARGET Florence K. conf on Whitsunday May 19 1907 by Alfred Rodman Hussey p 91
BARGET Katie conf on Whitsunday May 31 1903 by Alfred Rodman Hussey p 90
BARGET Lena conf on Easter Sunday 1900 p 88
BARGET Weston Robert son of   Barget, bapt in 1905 by Alfred Rodman
    Hussey, b Jun 9 1904 p 72
BARGET William H. b May 3 1914(?) or bapt on May 3 1914 by Alfred Rodman
    Hussey p 93
BARNEY Ann Elizabeth dau of William Bedford and Mary Barney bapt Oct 5 1822
    p 9
BARNEY Charlotte dau of William Bedford and Mary Barney bapt Apr 12 1825 p 13
BARNEY Frances Henry dau of William Bedford and Mary bapt Jan 14 1824 p 12
BARNEY Maria Munroe dau of William Bedford and Mary bapt on Mar 13 1821 p 6
BARNEY Samuel Chase son of William Bedford and Mary Barney b Oct 17 1819, bapt
    Nov 6 1819 p 4
BARNEY William Bedford hus of Mary and father of Samuel Chase p 4, Maria
    Munroe p 6, Ann Elizabeth p 9, Frances Henry p 12, Charlotte p 13
BARRETT Roswell m to Sarah J. Barrett on May 2 1854 p 114
BARRETT Sarah J. m to Roswell Barrett on May 2 1854 p 114
BARTLETT Adelheid Elizabeth dau of Alexander and Eleanora M. Bartlett b Mar 20
    1894, bapt Apr 22 1894 p 69
BARTLETT Alexander hus of Eleanora M., father of Adelheid Elizabeth p 69, Helen
    Belle p 74
BARTLETT Alice Riggs dau of G.W.B. and Amanda Griffith Bartlett, b Jan 2 1875,
    bapt May 16 1875 Whitsunday p 53
BARTLETT Amanda Griffith wife of G.W.B. Bartlett p 52
BARTLETT Caroline C.K. m to Charles Wyeth on Jul 16 1859 p 117
BARTLETT Eleanora wife of Alexander Bartlett p 74
BARTLETT G.W.B. hus of Amanda Griffith Bartlett, father of Vashti Rebecca p 52,
    Alice Riggs p 53, George Burnap p 55
BARTLETT George hus of Vashti Bartlett, father of Lucretia Vashti p 19, George
    Washington Burnap(?) p 19, Rebecca Carman p 24
BARTLETT George Burnap(?) son of G.W.B. and Amanda Griffith Bartlett, b Nov 13
    1877, bapt Jun 30 1878 p 55
BARTLETT George Washington Burnap(?) son of George and Vashti Bartlett, b Sep
    25 1834, bapt Jul 10 1835 p 19
BARTLETT George Washington Burnap(?) son of George and Vashti Bartlett, b Apr 7
    1843, bapt Dec 6 1843 p 29
BARTLETT(?) Harriet dau of Sally Ann Mudge and William Fay Knox, b Jun 6 1874,
    bapt Feb 13 1879 at 13(?) Boston Street p 55
BARTLETT Helen Belle dau of Alexander and Eleanora Bartlett, b Jan 23 1913,
    bapt Mar 2 1913 p 74
BARTLETT J. Alexander conf May 31 1914 by Alfred Rodman Hussey on Whitsunday
    p 93
BARTLETT Lucretia m to John Coborne on Mar 30 1828 p 103
BARTLETT Lucretia Vashti dau of George and Vashti Bartlett, b May 3 1827(?),
    bapt Jul 10 1835, m to Charles W.C. McCoy on May 3 1854 pp 19, 114

BARTLETT Mrs. on list of comm dated Sep 1869 p 81

BARTLETT Rebecca Carman dau of George and Vashti Bartlett, b Jan 12 1839, bapt Nov 19 1839 p 24

BARTLETT Vashti wife of George Bartlett p 19

BARTLETT Vashti Rebecca dau of G.W.B. and Amanda Griffith Bartlett, b Nov 15 1873, bapt Feb 27 1874 p 52

BARTON(?) Harriet dau of Sally Ann Mudge and William Fay Knox, b Jun 6 1874, bapt Feb 13 1879 at 13(?) Boston Street p 55

BASIL Jesse m to Harry T. Sedgwick, both of Baltimore on Apr 28 1919, Charles A Wing, officiating p 137

BAUHAN(Banhan?) Alexander E. of Holtwood PA m to Margaret E. Weldon of Baltimore on Feb 2 1918, Charles A. Wing, officiating p 137

BAYNE Mary Jane Campbell dau of Samuel and Mary Bayne, b Jun 12 1854, bapt Jan 16 1855 p 42

BAYNE Samuel and Mary p of Mary Jane Campbell p 42

BEAL B. Franklin m to Caroline E. Streeter on Oct 18 1855 p 115

BEASLEY Calvert (Myers) Beasley and Edward B. Beasley p of Mary Annette p 75

BEASLEY Edward Bailey m to Mary Calvert Myers, both of Baltimore, on May 19 1917, Charles A. Wing officiating p 137

BEASLEY Mary Annette dau of Calvert (Myers) Beasley and Edward B. Beasley, b Jun 9 1919, bapt Nov 2 1919 p 75

BECK Freddie conf on Whitsunday May 31 1903 by Alfred Rodman Hussey p 90

BELL Robert J. m to Ethel Pugh on Feb 26 1902, both of Norfolk VA, Alfred Rodman Hussey officiating at 1 West Hamilton Street p 134

BENDER Eleanora conf on May 31 1903 Whitsunday, Alfred Rodman Hussey officiating p 90

BENSON Sidney B. (or Brown Sidney B.) m to Nathaniel H. Monson on Dec 17 1842 p 109

BENTLY Sarah B. (of Montgomery County MD) m to William Lea Jr. on Jun 20 1867 p 122

BERNHARD Christina D. (or Christian) conf on Easter Sunday Apr 13 1884 during the ministry of Charles Richmond Weld p 85

BERNHARD John Leonard and Henrietta p of William Frederick p 58

BERNHARD Margaret conf and joined the church on Apr 14 1889, Palm Sunday p 86

BERNHARD Marie A. conf and joined the church on Apr 14 1889, Palm Sunday p 86

BERNHARD William Frederick son of Leonard and Henrietta Bernhard, b Dec 2 1879, bapt May 16 1880, Whitsunday p 58

BEVAN Mary B. (Benon Mary B.?) m to Sanderson Robert on Mar 28 1848 p 112

BINES Emily m Daniel Kraber on Apr 23 1833, both of Baltimore p 107

BINES Robert m to Saonica(?) Patterson on Jun 2 1836 p 107

BISHOP Adelene m to William G. Lloyd on Jan 15 1852 p 114

BLISS Harrison of Providence RI, m Caroline Wood of Baltimore on Aug 31 1918, Charles A. Wing, officiating p 137

BLOSSOM Frederick Augustus and Alice Sidney Morison Blossom p of Katherine Sidney p 73

BLOSSOM Katherine Sidney dau of Alice Sidney Morison Blossom and Frederick Augustus Blossom, b Nov 12 1905, bapt Nov 11 1910 at 911 North Charles Street p 73

BLUCHER George and Amelia p of Henrietta Blucher p 55

BLUCHER Henrietta dau of George and Amelia Blucher, b Mar 21 1877, bapt Nov 13 1877 at Stony Run p 55

BLUM Sophia of Reno NV, m to Henry N. Arnold of New York NY Feb 21 1914, Alfred Rodman Hussey officiating p 136

BOSLEY Amanda m to Ellridge G. Hall on May 19 1858 p 117

BOUGHMAN Frankie E. m to Louis F. Young on May 6 1875, both of Baltimore p 125

BOWLES Ben. F. m to Mary E. Bailey on Oct 22 1857 p 116

BRADFORD Henry B. m to Anne R. Garrett on Nov 9 1888 in the Unitarian Church in Wilmington DE, both of Wilmington p 128

BRADFORD Thomas Kell m to Jane Mayer on Jun 14 1883 at 16 McCullogh Street by Reverend Rush R. Shippen of Washington p 127

BRANDOW Melvin joined the church on Easter Sunday 1900 p 89

BRIGHAM Charles Pliny son of W.T. and M. Brigham, bapt in 1867 p 49

BRIGHAM Wales Cole son of William T. and Marian B. Brigham, b Jan 11 1870, bapt Mar 11 1870 at the home of William P. Cole, during the ministry of Reverend E.C. Guild p 50

BRIGHAM William T. and Marian B. both listed as comm in Sep 1869, p of Charles Pliny p 49, and Wales Cole p 50

BRINK Charles auf dem and Charlotte (Carrie) Veronica Schlens m on Apr 25 1894 Charles of Germantown MD; Charlotte of Baltimore, p of son b on May 21 1895 (name unknown) near Germantown in Montgomery County MD, bapt on Oct 1 1895 pp 70, 131

BROWN Caesar A. m Electa J. Rimph on Jun 13 1850 p 113

BROWN Esther A. m Francis Tiffany on Oct 14 1852 p 114

BROWN George and Hester p of John Cummings p 5

BROWN George J. and Esther, p of Robert Davison p 12

BROWN Harvey Ellicott bapt Dec 9 1858, adult p 46

BROWN Ida Jane dau of John J. and Mary Anne, b Apr 27 1846, bapt Dec 27 1846 p 32

BROWN John Cumming son of George and Hester Brown, b Jan 14 1821, bapt Mar 12 1821 p 5

BROWN John J. and Mary Anne Moore m Sep 15 1845, p of Ida Jane p 32, Minerva Roxana p 34, p 110

BROWN Minerva Roxana b-----, bapt Sep 24 1848 p 34

BROWN Robert Davison son of George J. and Esther Brown, bapt Jun 17 1824 p 12

BROWN Sidney B. (see Benson Sidney B.)

BROWN Thomas J. of Washington, m to Elsie Palmer of Baltimore on Oct 17 1894 p 131

BRUN Miss Eliza listed as a comm of the church after 1865 and prior to 1869 p 79

BRYANT Mary H. m to Henry Morton on Dec 28 1820 p 101

BUCKLER Ann Elizabeth m to Henry Rolando on Apr 29 1851 p 113

BUCKLER James son of John and Eliza Buckler, b May 4 1825, bapt Jun 29 1837 p 22

BUCKLER John son of John and Eliza Buckler, b Oct 28 1829, bapt Jun 29 1837 p 22

BUCKLER John and Eliza p of James p 22, Mary Teresa p 22, John p 22, Riggin p 22, Leslie Hepburn p 22

BUCKLER Leslie Hepburn child of John and Eliza Buckler, b Nov 1834, bapt Jun 29 1837 p 22

BUCKLER Mary Teresa dau of John and Eliza Buckler b Apr 6 1827, bapt June 29 1837 p 22

BUCKLER Riggin child of John and Eliza Buckler, b Nov 4 1831, bapt Jun 29 1837 p 22

BULL Frank W. of Pittsburg PA m Feb 22 1877 to Josephine G. Langren of Baltimore, C.K. Weld officiating p 125

BULLITT Alexander C. m to Mary D. Dennison on Dec 28 1824, both of Baltimore
    p 103
BURGESS Joshua m to Matilda J. McGowan on Oct 4 1853 p 114
BURGESS Mathilda J. m to George F. Granniss in Baltimore on Nov 1 1866, John
    F.W. Ware officiating p 121
BURGHEN Mary Van m to Daniel Mehrling on Sep 24 1891 both of Washington p 129
BURNAP Elizabeth Williams dau of George W. and Nancy W. Burnap, b Mar 28 1842,
    bapt Jul 3 1842, listed as a comm in Sep 1869 pp 27, 81
BURNAP George W. parish records kept by, pp 14, 104
BURNAP George W. and Nancy W.; George - keeper of church records pp 14, 104,
    p of Susan Williams p 18, Elizabeth Williams p 27; Nancy listed as a comm
    in Sep 1869 p 81
BURNAP Miss listed as a comm after 1865 and prior to 1869 p 79
BURNAP Mrs. listed as a comm after 1865 and prior to 1869 p 79
BURNAP Susan Williams dau of George W. and Nancy W. Burnap, b Oct 30 1833,
    bapt Jun 22 1834 p 18
BURNS Rev. Harry Foster, ministry:of baptisms p 76, funeral services p 98,
    marriage service p 138
BURNS Katie A. m to Jacob J.M. Nolan on Jun 29 1892, both of Shmokin PA p 130
BURTON John A. and Mary Burton p of Mary Elizabeth p 45
BURTON Mary Elizabeth dau of John A. and Mary Burton, b Aug 28 1857, bapt
    Apr 20 1858 p 45
BUTLER William B. m to Ann Maria Shaw on May 5 1858 p 116
BYRNE Edmond m to Flora C. Smith on Oct 5 1835,both of Baltimore p 107
CALLENDER William son of William and Mahitabel Callender, b May 10 1819, bapt
    Jun 1 1822 p 8
CALLENDER William and Mahitabel p of William Callender p 8
CALLOWHILL James C. of Boston, m to Gulli J. Oberg of Stockholm, Sweden, on
    Jun 1 1894 p 131
CAMPBELL Frank son of William and Susan Campbell, b Feb 14 1873, bapt Jan 14
    1874 at 108 McCulloch Street during the ministry of Charles Richmond Weld p 52
CAMPBELL Helen Foster conf and joined the church on Jun 6 1897 Whitsunday p 88
CAMPBELL Mildred J. conf on May 15 1910 Whitsunday by Alfred Rodman Hussey p 92
CAMPBELL William and Susan p of Frank Campbell p 52
CANAGA Mrs. A.B. (Ermina Can Canaga) conf on Good Friday Apr 3 1896, joined the
    church on Easter Apr 5 1896 p 87
CANBY Alice m Edward A. Robinson on Nov 14 1871 at the house of Thomas G. Canby
    in Dolphin Street at four p.m., E.C. Guild officiating p 123
CANBY Thomas G. home used for the marriage of Alice Canby and Edward A. Robinson
    on Nov 14 1871 in Dolphin Street, E.C. Guild officiating p 123
CARGET Joseph conf Jun 3 1906 Whitsunday by Alfred Rodman Hussey p 91
CARMAN Mrs. listed as a comm of the church in Sep 1869 p. 82
CARPENTER Moses S. m to Cidney Baldwin on Sep 27 1855 p 115
CARTER Alexander Maitland son of R.E. and   Carter, bapt on Sep 28 1823
    p 11
CARTER Frederick Augustus son of R.E. Carter and   Carter, bapt on Sep 28
    1823 p 11
CARTER Helen Maria dau of R.E. Carter and   Carter, bapt on Sep 28 1823 p 11
CARTER R.E. and   Carter p of Alexander Maitland p 11, Frederick Augustus
    p 11, Helen Maria p 11, William Henry p 11
CARTER William Henry son of R.E. Carter and   Carter, bapt on Sep 28 1823
    p 11

CASPARI Alice Clementina dau of Leslie Virginia and Charles Caspari Jr.,
    b Jun 27 1879, bapt Apr 1895 Palm Sunday the seventh, conf on Apr 12 1895
    Good Friday, joined the church on Easter Sunday Apr 14 1895 pp 70, 87
CASPARI Bertha dau of Charles and Leslie Virginia Caspari b May 14 1887,
    bapt May 15 1904, conf on Whitsunday May 22 1904 during the ministry of
    Alfred Rodman Hussey pp 72, 90
CASPARI Charles Jr. b May 11 1850, d Oct 13 1917, hus of Leslie Virginia,
    father of Alice Clementina pp 70, 87, Bertha p 72, Harriet Louise p 72,
    buried on Oct 15 1917, Pastor Hoffman officiating p 95
CASPARI Charles Jr. and Leslie Virginia p of Bertha p 72, Harriet Louise p 72,
    Alice Clementina pp 70, 87
CASPARI Frederick father of Nina p 134
CASPARI Harriet Louise dau of Charles Jr. and Leslie Virginia, b Feb 11 1892,
    bapt May 15 1904, conf on Easter Sunday Apr 27 1912, Alfred Rodman Hussey
    officiating pp 72, 93
CASPARI Nina dau of (the late) Frederick Caspari of Baltimore, m John G.
    Oglesby of Atlanta GA on Nov 9 1907 at 7 p.m. in Govans, Baltimore County,
    Alfred Rodman Hussey officiating p 134
CATE Amelia B. m Henry James on Feb 20 1851 p 113
CATE Georgiana B. m to Henry W. Heird on Nov 15 1853 p 114
CHAMBERLAIN Frances E. m to John R. Hynson on Sep 6 1832 p 106
CHAMBERLAIN Reverend L.P. pastor of N.E. Church Chicago, bapt Emma Rosalie,
    child of Edward C. and Emma M. Guild, at the home of the pastor on Dec 19
    1869 p 50
CHAMBERLAIN Reverend N(athan) H. marriages performed by, p 119
CHAMBERLAIN Reverend N(athan) H. bapt Annie May Keith, b Mar 12 1862, dau of
    Edward M. and Maria Keith, bapt on Oct 26 1862 p 48
CHANDLER George H. and Elvira S. p of Samuel Coffin, b Nov 13 1875, bapt
    Jan 17 1876 p 54
CHANDLER Samuel Coffin son of George H. and Elvira S. Chandler, b Nov 13 1875,
    bapt Jan 17 1876 p 54
CHASE Algernon Sidney son of Algernon Sidney and Mary Augusta Chase, b Nov 13
    1844, bapt Nov 16 1845 p 31
CHASE Algernon Sidney and Mary Augusta p of George Thomsen p 31, Emily Forbes
    p 31, Algernon Sidney p 31, Lewis Simmonds p 46, Edward Linzee (Lindsey)
    p 46, Annie Augusta and Mary Tilden, twins, p 46
CHASE Annie Augusta dau of Algernon Sidney and Mary Augusta Chase (twin of
    Mary Tilden), b Jul 27 1850, bapt Oct 31 1858 p 46
CHASE Edward Linzee (Lindsey) son of Algernon Sidney and Mary Augusta Chase,
    b Jun 19 1847, bapt Oct 31 1858 p 46
CHASE Emily Forbes dau of Algernon Sidney and Mary Augusta Chase, b Sep 16
    1840, bapt Nov 16 1845 p 31
CHASE George Thomsen son of Algernon Sidney and Mary Augusta Chase, b Aug 14
    1838, bapt Nov 16 1845 p 31
CHASE Lewis Simonds son of Algernon Sidney and Mary Augusta Chase, b Mar 14
    1846, bapt Oct 31 1858 p 46
CHASE Mary Tilden dau of Algernon Sidney and Mary Augusta Chase (twin of Annie
    Augusta Chase), b Jul 27 1850, bapt Oct 31 1858 p 46
CHIPMAN Florence Weld dau of Marcus M. and Sarah Jane Chipman, b Sep 1 1878,
    bapt Jul 3 1879 at 88 Baltimore Street p 57
CHIPMAN George and Jane Ann p of Mary Chipman p 60, Jennie White Chipman p 60
CHIPMAN Helen Marcus dau of Marcus M(orton) and Sarah Jane Chipman, b Apr 10
    1881, bapt Apr 10 1887 Easter Sunday p 62

CHIPMAN Jennie White dau of George and Jane Ann Chipman, b 1863, bapt Apr 6
1884 Palm Sunday p 60

CHIPMAN Marcus M(orton) and Sarah Jane p of Florence Weld p 57, Helen Marcus
p 62

CHIPMAN Mary dau of George and Jane Ann Chipman, b 1859, bapt Apr 6 1884
Palm Sunday p 60

CHUBB Emily W. m to Cephas Dodd McFarland on Nov 2 1865, both of Baltimore,
John F.W. Ware officiating p 121

CHUBB Mrs. listed as a comm of the church in Sep 1869 p 81

CLAP Aaron and Ann p of George Clark p 7, Sarah Ann p 7, Francis Augustus p 7

CLAP Francis Augustus son of Aaron and Ann Clap, b Sep 25 1820, bapt Jun 3
1821 p 7

CLAP George Clark son of Aaron and Ann Clap, b Jan 13 1814, bapt Jun 3 1821
p 7

CLAP Sarah Ann dau of Aaron and Ann Clap, b Aug 20 1818, bapt Jun 3 1821,
m George Hyde of Boston on Sep 17 1839 pp 7,108

CLAPP Charles W. and Mary A. p of Corrina Breed Clapp p 43

CLAPP Corrina Breed dau of Charles W. and Mary A. Clapp, b Sep 9 1855, bapt
Apr 12 1856 p 43

CLARK Reverend C.C. officiated at the funeral service of Angeline W. Sumner,
b Jun 3 1834, died Jan 19 1920, funeral on Jan 21 1920 p 97

CLEVELAND Anthony B. and Mary p of William Charles p 24, Clement p 29, Mary
Manning p 33

CLEVELAND Clement son of Anthony B. and Mary Cleveland, b Sep 29 1843, bapt
May 19 1844 p 29

CLEVELAND Mary Manning dau of Anthony B. and Mary Cleveland, b Oct 11 1846,
bapt Sep 29 1847 p 33

CLEVELAND William Charles son of Anthony B. and Mary Cleveland, b Jul 5 1839,
bapt Jul 21 1839 p 24

CLIFFE Henry m to Angelina Finley on Oct 30 1828, both of Baltimore p 104

COALE Isaac m Mary Gable on Apr 30 1851 p 113

COLCELL, Anna M. m Walter F. Stutz on Dec 30 1919, both of Washington DC,
Charles A. Wing officiating p 137

COLE Channing Burnap son of William P. and Emiline Cole, b Jul 4 1850, bapt
Oct 20 1850 p 36

COLE Charles Pliny son of William P. and Emiline Cole, b Mar 20 1845, bapt
Dec 14 1845 p 31

COLE Donald son of George B. and Mary J. (Williams) Cole, b Dec 29 1885, bapt
May 19 1886, Wednesday, at 44 Linden Avenue p 61

COLE E. V. listed as a communicant of the church after 1865 and prior to
Sep 1869 p 78

COLE Edith dau of George Byron and Mary J. (Williams) Cole, b Jun 5 1881, bapt
Nov 24 1881, Thanksgiving Day, at 196 Saint Paul Street p 58

COLE Edward Curtis son of William R. and Mary L. Cole, b Mar 28 1867, bapt
Jun 21 1867 p 49

COLE Edwin Curtis son of William P. and Emiline Cole, b Jun 25 1835, bapt
Jan 1 1837 p 21

COLE Eleanor Parker dau of John R. and Margaret P. Cole, b Feb 2 1836, bapt
Jan 1 1837 p 21

COLE Emiline dau of William R. and Marie Elizabeth Cole, b Jan 11 1856, bapt
Jun 1 1856 p 43

COLE Miss Flora E. listed as a comm of the church on Jan 1 1871 p 82

COLE Florence Baker dau of William P. and Emiline Cole, b Jul 21 1842, bapt
   Dec 8 1842 p 27
COLE Francis Osborn son of William P. and Emiline Cole, b Jul 2 1840, bapt
   June 6 1844 p 25
COLE George Byron and Mary J. (Williams) Cole, p of Edith p 58, Natalie p 61,
   Donald p 61, Ralph Neff p 64
COLE Helen May dau of Reverend Moo(e)re and Elizabeth S. Latham Cole, received
   communion during the first regular service held in the reconstructed church
   Nov 5 1893 p 67
COLE Hore Esther dau of William P. and Emiline Cole, b Feb 12 1847, bapt
   May 9 1847 p 33
COLE Howard Beatty son of William R. and M.E. Cole, b Mar 7 1873, bapt Jun 30
   1873 during the ministry of Charles Richmond Weld p 52
COLE John R. m to Margaret R. McGinn on Mar 31 1835 both of Baltimore p 107
COLE John R. and Margaret P. p of Eleanor Parker p 21
COLE Margaret Roswell dau of William R. and Maria E. Cole, b Aug 20 1858,
   bapt Jan 9 1859 p 46
COLE Mrs. Maria E. listed as a comm of the church in Sep 1869 p 81
COLE Marion Billings dau of William P. and Emiline Cole, b Oct 19 1838, bapt
   Mar 10 1839 p 23
COLE May dau of William R. and Maria E. Cole, bapt Jan 9 1870 at the home of
   William R. Cole, during the ministry of E.C. Guild p 50
COLE May m to Frank Loring Nichols of Washington DC at the home of the bride's
   mother in Mount Washington, Baltimore County, on Feb 17 1904 at 6:15 p.m.,
   Alfred Rodman Hussey officiating, dau of Maria E. and the late William R.
   Cole p 133
COLE Reverend Moo(e)re and Elizabeth S. Latham Cole p of Helen May Cole p 67
COLE Natalie dau of George B. and Mary J. (Williams) Cole, b Feb 9 1854, bapt
   Jun 5 1884 at 196 Saint Paul Street p 61
COLE Ralph Neff son of George B. and Mary J. Cole, b Jun 25 1889, bapt Jan 12
   1890 at 1821 Linden Avenue p 64
COLE W.R. listed as a comm of the church after 1865 p 79
COLE William P. listed as a comm of the church after 1865 and again in Sep
   1869 p 78, 81
COLE William P. and Emiline p of Edwin Curtis p 21, William Roswell p 17,
   Marion Billings p 23, Francis Osborn p 25, Florence Baker p 27, Charles
   Pliny p 31, Hore Esther p 33, Channing Burnap p 36
COLE William R. m to Maria E. Muncks on Nov 7 1854 p 115
COLE William R. and Maria Elizabeth p of Emiline p 43, Margaret Roswell p 46,
   May p 50, Howard Beatty p 52
COLE William R., Reverend, officiated at the wedding of Charles Louis Welke
   and Mary Louise Rixse on Sep 25 1898; Reverend Cole was from Cohasset, MA
   at the time p 132
COLE William Roswell son of W.R. Cole and M.L. Cole, b Feb 14 1865, bapt
   Jul 1 1865 p 48
COLE William Roswell son of William P(arker) and Emiline Cole, b May 23 1831,
   bapt Mar 4 1832 p 17
COLEMAN Mollie L. conf by Alfred Rodman Hussey on Whitsunday Jun 11 1905 p 91
COLEMAN (Reverend W.) officiated at baptisms on Nov 8 1818 the Sunday after the
   dedication of the church p 2
CONANT Sherman m to Frances Dewry of Baltimore on Jan 14 1807 by John F.W.
   Ware; Sherman Conant was from Tallahassee FL p 122

CONNAC Margaret More of Belfast, Ireland, m to John Rose of Philadelphia PA
   on May 19 1909 at 1:15 p.m. at 1314 Bolton Street, Alfred Rodman Hussey
   officiating p 135
CONNER Ann R. m to Richard M. Renick on Jun 15 1841 p 109
CONTEE Alice Lee dau of Louis and Elizabeth (Travers) Contee, b Dec 11 1891,
   bapt Easter Sunday Apr 5 1896 p 70-1/2
CONTEE Carrie Hester dau of Louis and Martha Elizabeth (Travers) Contee,
   b Oct 14 1886, bapt Apr 10,Easter Sunday,1887 p 61
CONTEE Elizabeth Hall dau of Louis and Elizabeth Contee, b Mar 31 1889,
   bapt Mar 29 1891, Easter Sunday p 65
CONTEE Louis and Martha Elizabeth (Travers) Contee p of Carrie Hester p 61,
   Elizabeth Hall p 65, Alice Lee p 70-1/2
COOLIDGE Eliza Ann(e) dau of William and   Coolidge, bapt Jul 4 1819 p 3
COOLIDGE Joshua W. of Baltimore, m to Anna C. Myers of Pen Mar PA on Feb 11
   1912 at 2:15 p.m. at 1314 Bolton Street, Alfred Rodman Hussey officiating
   p 135
COOLIDGE William and wife, p of Eliza Ann(e) p 3
COON Delia A. m to William U. Morris on Nov 28 1847 p 112
COOPER Cora Ida conf on Jun 8 1878 during the ministry of Charles Richmond
   Weld p 85
CORNER Annette m to James Edwin Myers on Mar 31 1883 at the residence of
   Mr. Solomon Corner, corner of Calvert and Biddle Streets p 126
CORNER Solomon marriage of Annette Corner took place at his residence on
   the corner of Calvert and Biddle Streets Mar 31 1883 to James Edwin
   Myers p 126
COY Sarah E. m to Erwin Merrifield on Jun 25 1866 in Baltimore by John F.W.
   Ware p 121
CRANCH John m to Charlotte D. Appleton on Apr 15 1845 p 110
CRESSAR Alice Clementina--see Caspari, Alice C. pp 70, 87
CRESSAR Leslie Virginia and Charles Jr.--see Caspari, Leslie Virginia and
   Charles Jr. p 72
CROOKER Reverend Henry, D.D. officiated at the funeral of Ludlow Lilly on
   Jan 18 1921 (b May 27 1874, d Jan 14 1921), Reverend Crooker served after
   the resignation of Charles A. Wing and before the arrival of Reverend
   Wing's successor p 97
CRUMPTON Claribel B. of Baltimore, m to Lewis H. Gibson of Zanesville, OH
   on Dec 20 1893 at 4 p.m. on East Mount Royal Avenue, A. D. Smith asst. p 130
CUGLE Miss C. listed as a comm of the church after 1865 and prior to Sep
   1869 p 78
CUGLE Caroline Augusta of Baltimore, m to Richard Henry Atwell of York(?)
   on Apr 15 1841 p 109
CUGLE Fannie dau of John Cugle and wife, b Dec 13 1837, bapt Mar 1843 p 28
CUGLE Miss H. listed as a comm of the church after 1865 and prior to
   Sep 1869 p 78
CUGLE John and wife p of Fanny p 28, John Plaskitt p 28
CUGLE John Plaskitt son of John Cugle and wife, b Jun 26 1839, bapt Mar
   1843 p 28
CUGLE Miss listed as a comm of the church after 1865 and prior to Sep 1869
   p 79
CUNNINGHAM Abbie E. m to John W. Wright on Jun 4 1856 p 116
CUNNINGHAM Lavinia m to Henry Dundore on Jan 10 1856 p 115
CUNNINGHAM Mary m to George Oliver on Sep 6 1846 p 111

CURLET John and wife p of Milton p 3
CURLET Milton son of John Curlet and wife, bapt Jun 13 1819 p 3
DALEY Elizabeth Margaret dau of Joshua Daley, bapt Nov 27 1828 p 14
DALEY Henry Hall son of Joshua Daley, bapt Nov 27 1828 p 14
DALEY Joshua father of Elizabeth Margaret p 14, Joshua Burnap p 14, Henry Hall
    p 14
DALEY Joshua Burnap son of Joshua Daley, bapt Nov 27 1828 p 14
DALL Austin son of James and Henrietta Dall, b in Baltimore County Jun 3
    1816(?), bapt Oct 3 1819 p 4
DALL James and Henrietta p of William Holly p 2, Austin p 4, Joseph Edward
    p 12, William p 13, Maria Louisa p 16
DALL Joseph Edward son of James and Henrietta Dall, b Aug 13 1823, bapt
    Apr 30 1824 p 12
DALL Maria Louisa dau of James and Henrietta Dall, bapt Jun 15 1831 p 16
DALL William son of James and Henrietta Dall, b Aug 28 1824, bapt Apr 6
    1825 p 13
DALL William Holly son of James and Henrietta Dall, b in Baltimore County
    Sep 4 1817, bapt Nov 8 1818 by Mr. Colman on the Sunday after the
    dedication of the church p 2
DARLEY Laura R. m to Joseph C. Manning on Jan 6 1874 at the church on the
    corner of Charles and Franklin Streets at 1 p.m. p 125
DAUBERT Dora conf and joined the church on Palm Sunday Apr 14 1889, d Monday
    Mar 30 1903 p 86
DAUBERT Kate conf and joined the church on Palm Sunday Apr 14 1889 p 86
DAVIS August and James Madison (called Mattie) Simon Davis p of Leslie Davis
    p 56
DAVIS Frank M. b 1866, d Dec 19 1918, funeral Dec 21 1918, Charles A. Wing
    officiating p 95
DAVIS Leslie son of Ausust and James Madison (called Mattie) Simon Davis,
    b Dec 2 1878, bapt May 22 1879 at 50 Franklin Street p 56
DAWES George father of Mary Elizabeth p 15
DAWES Harrison and Lucy p of Lucy Cranch p 7, Mary Greenleaf p 12, John
    Greenleaf p 15
DAWES John Greenleaf son of Harrison and Lucy Dawes, bapt May 31 1829 p 15
DAWES Lucy Cranch dau of Harrison and Lucy Dawes, bapt Sep 23 1821 p 7
DAWES Mary Elizabeth dau of George Dawes and wife, bapt May 31 1829 p 15
DAWES Mary Greenleaf dau of Harrison and Lucy Dawes, bapt Jul 12 1824,
    F.W.P. Greenwood officiating p 12
DAWES Thomas son of Thomas and Elizabeth Dawes, b in Baltimore Mar 11 1818,
    bapt Nov 8 1818 p 2
DAWES Thomas and Elizabeth p of Thomas p 2
DAY William Cathcart, Ph.D. m to Jeannie Learny(Leamy?) on Dec 27 1884, in
    the church at 5:30 p.m. p 127
DEAN Grove Parker son of Grove Parker and Dorothy Sweeting (Mudge) Dean, b
    Jul 23 1918, bapt Dec 29 1918 during the ministry of Charles A. Wing p 75
DEAN Grove Parker and Dorothy Sweeting (Mudge) Dean m May 29 1915 at 12 noon
    at 1752 Park Avenue, Alfred R. Hussey officiating, p of Grove Parker Jr.
    pp 75, 136
DELANO Mr. father of Salame p 15
DELANO Salome dau of Mr. Delano, bapt May 10 1837 in Washington p 15
DEMARTELLO Charles Frank and Elizabeth p of Isobella p 70-1/2, Leona
    Eliziebethe(?) p 63, May Elizabeth p 70

DE MARTELLO Isabella dau of Charles Frank and Elizabeth De Martello, b Dec 9
    1879, bapt Apr 16 1897, Good Friday, in the church p 70-1/2

DE MARTELLO Leona Eliziebethe b Jan 17 1889, bapt Jun 9 1889 in the church,
    on Whitsunday, m Charles Handler on Jan 18 1911 at 7:30 p.m. in the church,
    both of Baltimore, Alfred R. Hussey officiating pp 63, 135

DE MARTELLO May Elizabeth dau of Charles Frank and Elizabeth De Martello,
    b May 15 1894, bapt Jun 2 1895, Whitsunday, in the church p 70

DENNISON Mary D. m Alexander C. Bullitt on Dec 28 1824, both of Baltimore p 103

DEWRY Frances m to Sherman Conant of Tallahassee FL on Jan 14 1867 by John
    F.W. Ware p 122

DICKINSON Herbert M. m to Beulah M. Miller on Jun 5 1893 at 12 noon in the
    chapel p 130

DIXON Herbert E. m Anna C. Kahn in the church on Nov 4 1911 at 11:30 a.m.,
    both of Hershey PA, Alfred R. Hussey officiating p 135

DOAN Rev. Frank C. officiated at the funeral of George Whitelock, b Dec 25
    1854, d Jan 8 1920, funeral service Jan 10 1920 after the resignation of
    Charles A. Wing and before the arrival of his successor p 97

DONALDSON James Lowry son of Mr. R.K. Lowry, bapt May 12 1819 p 3

DOWD Winifred V. m to Frederick A. George Jan 20 1915 at 3:15 p.m. in the
    chapel, both of Baltimore, Alfred R. Hussey officiating p 136

DOWED Beata M. conf on Whitsunday May 22 1904 by Alfred Rodman Hussey p 90

DOWNING Martha A. m to George N. Mackenzie on Jul 11 1850 p 113

DU FORT Leon C. m to Elizabeth J. Fanning on March 16 1912 at 11:30 a.m. at
    1 West Hamilton Street, both of Baltimore, Alfred R. Hussey officiating
    p 135

DUNDORE Henry m to Lavinia Cunningham on Jan 10 1856 p 115

DURHAM Rebecca G. m to Mr. Hugh Gelston on Jul 8 1828, both of Baltimore p 104

DUSHANE Charles B. m to Jennie W. Chipman on Apr 30 1889 at 8:00 p.m. in the
    church, both of Baltimore p 128

EASTMAN Edith M. m to Guy B. Stuart on Jan 12 1875 at the church at 6:30 p.m.,
    both of Baltimore, C.K. Weld officiating p 125

EATON Frances dau of Geoge N. and Susan B. Eaton, b Dec 8 1858, bapt Nov 25
    1858 p 46

EATON George N. listed as a comm of the church after 1865 and prior to 1869,
    m to Susan B. Mayhew on Apr 22 1844 pp 79, 81, 110

EATON George N. and Susan B. Mayhew Eaton, p of Susan p 33, Mary Matilda p 34,
    Maria Lovell p 36, William Mayhew p 41, Susan Mayhew p 46, Frances p 46

EATON Maria Lovell dau of George N. and Susan Eaton, b Jan 22 1850, bapt
    Oct 13 1850 p 36

EATON Mary Matilda dau of George N. and Susan B. Eaton, b Jan 5 1849, bapt
    Mar 19 1849 p 34

EATON Susan dau of George N. and Susan B. Eaton, b Sep 20 1847, bapt Mar 5
    1848 p 33

EATON Mrs. Susan B. listed as a comm of the church in Sep 1869 p 81

EATON Susan Mayhew dau of George N. and Susan B. Mayhew, b Dec 5 1857, bapt
    Nov 25 1858 p 46

EATON William Mayhew son of George N. and Susan B. Eaton, b Dec 12 1853, bapt
    May 14 1854 p 41

EBERMAN Norman E. listed as conf on May 31 1903, Whitsunday, Alfred Rodman
    Hussey officiating p 90

EGBERT Daniel and Caroline M. Egbert p of Virginia p 37, Emma Kate p 37

EGBERT Emma Kate dau of Daniel and Caroline M. Egbert, b Jul 31 1849, bapt
    Mar 9 1851 p 37

EGBERT Virginia dau of Daniel and Caroline M. Egbert, b Sep 15 1845, bapt
   Mar 9 1851 p 37
EISENBRANDT C. Henry b Feb 9 1861, d Apr 11 1919, Charles A. Wing officiating
   p 96
EISENBRANDT Mrs. C. Henry conf on Whitsunday May 30 1909 by Alfred Rodman
   Hussey p 92
ELIOT Elizabeth Margaret dau of Mr. and Mrs. Eliot of Washington bapt Jun 24
   1821 in Washington DC p 7
ELIOT Mr. and Mrs. of Washington DC p of Elizabeth Margaret p 7
ELLSWORTH Elmer son of Martin and Louisa League Ellsworth, b Aug 25 1891, bapt
   Apr 28 1893, Rev. Charles T. Sempers officiating p 66
ELLSWORTH Florence dau of Martin and Louisa League Ellsworth, b Sep 22 1889,
   bapt Apr 28 1893 in the chapel, Rev. Charles T. Sempers officiating p 66
ELLSWORTH Martin and Louisa League p of Florence p 66, Elmer p 66
EMERSON George F. m to Augusta A. Whittier on Apr 21 1851 p 113
EMMART Bessie dau of P. Thomas and Helena C. Emmart, b Nov 20 1880, bapt
   Apr 10 1887, Easter Sunday, in church, m to Samuel Hamburger on Sep 29 1904,
   5:30 p.m. at 219 West Lafayette Avenue, both of Baltimore p 134
EMMART Georgia m to Charles R. Rauch on Feb 26 1889 at 1326 Argyle Avenue,
   both of Baltimore p 128
EMMART Helen b 1874, d Apr 4 1918, buried Apr 6 1918, Charles A. Wing
   officiating p 95
EMMART P. Thomas and Helena C. Emmart p of Bessie p 61
ENDICOT George m to Miss Sarah Lee Munroe on Dec 18 1828 p 105
ENDICOTT William m to Mary E. Munroe on May 20 1845 p 110
ENGLAND Katherine conf on Easter Sunday 1900 p 88
ENGLAND Mamie conf on Easter Sunday 1900 p 88
EULER Pranz m in the church at 6 p.m. Nov 16 1887 to Lillie Salzer p 127
EVERETT Mr. of Hallowell MA, m John R. Howard to Caroline Jarvis, both of
   Baltimore on Jul 28 1827 p 104
FANNING Elizabeth J. m to Leon C. Du Fort on Mar 16 1912 at 11:30 a.m., at
   1 West Hamilton Street, Alfred Rodman Hussey officiating p 135
FERNALD, Hentey T. of Massachusetts, m to Minna R. Simon, dau of Charles and
   Helen Simon of Baltimore, on Jun 9 1890 at 8 p.m. at 1119 Linden Avenue p 129
FIELD Abeather(?) W. m to Penelope I. Healey on Sep 8 1856 p 116
FINLEY Angelina m to Henry Cliffe on Oct 30 1828, both of Baltimore p 104
FITCH Emily R. conf on Whitsunday May 22 1904, Alfred Rodman Hussey officiating
   p 90
FLODT Adeline conf and joined the church on Palm Sunday Apr 14 1889 p 86
FONDE Charles Henry son of the Widow E. Fonde, b Jan 1 1827, bapt Jul 19 1833
   p 18
FONDE Sarah Jane b Oct 9 1825, bapt Jul 19 1833, dau of the Widow E. Fonde p 18
FONDE Widow E. mother of Sarah Jane p 18, Charles Henry p 18
FORBES George m to Sarah Watson on Oct 30 1850 p 113
FORBES James son of James and Sarah Forbes, b Jul 31 1851, bapt Sep 8 1851 p 38
FORBES James and Sarah Watson Forbes p of James p 38, Richard Harvey p 41,
   Prudence Watson p 44
FORBES Prudence Watson dau of James and Sarah Watson Forbes, b Nov 7 1856,
   bapt Dec 9 1856 p 44
FORBES Richard Harvey son of James and Sarah Forbes, b Sep 23 1854, bapt
   Sep 31 1854 p 41
FOSTER Catharine dau of John M. and Louisa Foster, b Mar 11 1820, bapt May 19
   1822 by the Reverend Jared Sparks pp 1, 8

FOSTER George Presbury son of John M. and Louisa Foster, b Nov 29 1818, bapt
   May 19 1822 by the Reverend Jared Sparks pp 1,8
FOSTER James Forbes son of John M. and Louisa Foster, b Oct 19 1821, bapt
   May 19 1822 by the Reverend Jared Sparks pp 1, 8
FOSTER John M. and Louisa p of George Presbury pp 1, 8, Catharine pp 1, 8,
   James Forbes pp 1, 8
FOWLER Florence M. m Aquila B. Murray on Feb 8 1821, both of Baltimore p 102
FOYER Louisa H. m to Richard Mott on Mar 1 1831, both of Baltimore p 105
FRANCE Joseph son of Joseph C. and Roberta Lee (Simon) France, b in Baltimore
   Aug 30 1893, bapt Jan 18 1894 at 1706 John Street p 68
FRANCE Joseph C. m to Roberta Lee Simon dau of Adolphe and Margaret Torney
   Simon of Baltimore on Sep 24 1892 at 11:15 a.m. in the chapel p 130
FRANCE Joseph C. and Roberta Lee Simon France p of Joseph p 68
FREDRIKSEN Ida m to Walter S.(?) Hamburger on May 22 1905 at 11 a.m. at 209
   North Broadway, both of Baltimore, Alfred Rodman Hussey officiating p 134
FREEBURGER Edwin R. m to Theresa J. Phillips on Jul 8 1885 at 6 p.m. in the
   church p 127
FREEBURGER Edwin Railly and Theresa Johanna (Phillips) Freeburger p of
   Minnie Ada p 61
FREEBURGER Fred conf on May 22 1904 Whitsunday by Alfred Rodman Hussey p 90
FREEBURGER Minnie Ada dau of Edwin Railly and Theresa Johanna (Phillips)
   Freeburger, b Nov 13 1886, bapt Jan 23 1887 p 61
FREEMAN Clarke F. on Providence Road, m to Elizabeth Wood on Feb 1 1919,
   (Miss Wood of Baltimore), Charles A. Wing officiating p 137
FREEMAN Sophia Price m to John Le Messurier Smith on Jan 27 1829 p 105
FREIS Philip C. listed as a comm of the church on Sep 1869 p 82
FRICK Elizabeth A. m to William Power on Oct 14 1847 p 112
FRICK Francis son of William and Mary Frick, bapt on Feb 1 1830 p 15
FRICK James Sloan son of William and Mary Frick, b Jun 10 1833, bapt Apr 1834
   p 18
FRICK Mary Lindsay dau of William and Mary Frick, bapt Dec 17 1822 p 9
FRICK William son of William and Mary Frick born Jul 15 1835, bapt Oct 9 1835
   p 20
FRICK William and Mary p of Mary Lindsay p 9, Francis p 15, James Sloan p 18,
   William p 20
FRIEBUS (Frisbur?) Rosetta G. of Washington DC, m to William C. Sherwood, of
   New York on Jan 22 1912 at 12 M., at 103 Beechdale Road, Roland Park MD,
   Alfred Rodman Hussey officiating p 135
FRIEZE Julia Antoinette dau of Philip C. and Harriet Frieze, b Oct 2 1853,
   bapt Apr 17 1856 p 43
FRIEZE Philip C. and Harriet Frieze p of Julia Antoinette p 43, Philip Henry
   p 43
FRIEZE Philip Henry son of Philip C. and Harriet Frieze, b Jan 26 1856, bapt
   Apr 17 1856 p 43
FRIEZE Rebecca (Mrs.) m to William Tufts on Sep 13 1832, both of Baltimore
   p 106
GABLE Mary m to Isaac Coale on Apr 30 1851 p 113
GADO Albert Frederick son of Henry and Lena C. F. Gado, b Jan 25 1891, bapt
   Apr 26 1891 p 65
GADO Henry and Lena C.F. Gado p of Albert Frederick p 65
GAITHER Evan of Baltimore County m to Sarah Ann Shipley of Westminster on
   Nov 1 1831 p 106
GAMBRILL Charles A. and ----- Gambrill p of George Bancroft p 48

GAMBRILL George Bancroft son of Charles A. and ------Gambrill, bapt Oct 3 1866
p 48

GARDNER Frank Streetes son of Julia Streetes Gardner and Henry Gardner, b
Dec 9 1916, bapt Jun 5 1921 p 76

GARDNER Henry and Julia Streetes Gardner p of Julia Goodal p 74, Frank
Streetes p 76

GARDNER Julia Goodal dau of Julia S. Gardner and Henry Gardner, b at White
Plains NY Nov 24 1912, bapt in church May 30 1915 p 74

GARRETT Anne R. m to Henry B. Bradford on Nov 9 1888 in the Unitarian Church
in Wilmington DE at 6 p.m., both of Wilmington p 128

GAYLE Lieut. Edward E. m to Mary Bartlett Ayres on Mar 9 1881 at the U.S.
Barracks, Washington DC, headquarters of General Ayres U.S.A. p 126

GELSTON Edward Hardy son of Hugh and Rebecca Gelston, b Sep 15 1833, bapt
Nov 10 1835 p 20

GELSTON Georgiana dau of Hugh and Rebecca Gelston, bapt Jun 15 1831 p 16

GELSTON Georgine S. (Georgiana?) m to Isaac D. Jones on Jul 20 1847 p 111

GELSTON Hugh listed as a comm of the church in Sep 1869, m to Rebecca G.
Durham on Jul 8 1828, both of Baltimore pp 81, 104

GELSTON Hugh and Rebecca p of Edward Hardy p 20, Georgiana p 16, Hugh Duckaw
p 16, Martha Hardy p 17, Rebecca Gwynn p 20, Isabel p 23, Robert Bruce p 23,
Victor Delaunay p 25, Rebecca Elise p 26, Juliet Therese p 28

GELSTON Hugh Duckaw bapt Jun 15 1831 p 16

GELSTON Isabel dau of Hugh and Rebecca Gelston, b Jun 17 1836, bapt Mar 18
1839 p 23

GELSTON Juliet Therese dau of Hugh and Rebecca Gelston, b Dec 17 1842, bapt
Apr 5 1843 p 28

GELSTON Kate (see Gelston, Isabel) p 23

GELSTON Martha Hardy dau of Hugh and Rebecca Gelston, b Dec 6 1831, bapt
Apr 26 1833 p 17

GELSTON Rebecca Elise dau of Hugh and Rebecca Gelston, b May 27 1841, bapt
Jun 22 1841 p 26

GELSTON Rebecca Gwynn dau of Hugh and Rebecca Gelston, b --- 13 1835, bapt
Nov 10 1835, listed as a comm of the church in Sep 1869 pp 20, 81

GELSTON Robert Bruce son of Hugh and Rebecca Gelston, b Nov 17 1837, bapt
Mar 18 1839 p 23

GELSTON Victor Delaunay son of Hugh and Rebecca Gelston, b Mar 27 1839, bapt
Feb 29 1840 p 25

GEOGHEGAN Reverend William B. of Berkeley CA, officiated at the baptism of
Melvin Louis Welke, son of Charles Louis and Mary Louise Welke, b Sep 24
1899, bapt Sunday Oct 29 1899 p 71

GEORGE Frederick A. m Winifred V. Dowd on Jan 20 1915 at the chapel at 3:15
p.m., both of Baltimore p 136

GEORGII Fred. (see also George, Frederick A.) conf on Easter Sunday 1900 p 88

GERELIUS Reverend Charles G. (see also Girelius, Reverend Charles G.) pp 77,
138

GESIGER Paul E. (see also Geseger, Paul E.) m to Ella Jautsch on Jun 8 1925
by Reverend Charles G. Girelius, both of Baltimore, at his residence p 138

GIBSON Lewis H. of Zanesville OH m Claribel B. Crumpton of Baltimore, on
Dec 20 1893 at 4 p.m., A. D. Smith Asst. p 130

GILDERSLEEVE Mrs. listed as a comm of the church in 1865 p 78

GIRELIUS Reverend Charles G. officiated at the baptism of Carl Vietor Nitze,
son of Carl L. Nitze and Mathilda V. Nitze, Carl Vietor was born on Jun 26
1925 and bapt on Sep 27 1925; m Paul E. Gesiger and Etta Jautsch, both of
Baltimore, on Jun 8 1925 at his residence pp 77, 138

GMINDER Albert J. m Lillian V. Mills, both of Baltimore, on Jul 7 1890 at
9:30 a.m. in the church p 129

GMINDER Albert J. and Lillian V. (Mills) p of Rose Elizabeth p 71, Albert
Roland p 67

GMINDER Albert Roland (see also Grunder, Albert R.) son of Albert Jacob and
Lillian Viola (Mills) Gminder of Baltimore, bapt May 23 1893, Whitsunday
p 67

GMINDER Lillian V. (Mills) b Sep 19 1862, d Apr 6 1919, funeral Apr 8 1919,
Charles A. Wing officiating p 96

GMINDER Roland (see also Grinder, Roland) conf on Easter Sunday Apr 16 1911,
by Alfred Rodman Hussey p 92

GMINDER Rose Elizabeth (see also Grinder, Rose E.) dau of Albert J. and
Lillian V. (Mills) Gminder, b Jul 24 1892, bapt Jan 2 1898 (first child
christened in the new baptismal font), conf Easter Sunday Apr 27 1912 by
Alfred Rodman Hussey pp 71, 93

GODMAN John D. m Angelica Peale on Oct 6 1821, both of Baltimore p 102

GOOD Catherine Elizabeth m Volney E. Howard on Mar 6 1837 at Washington p 107

GOODENOW Frances J. of Baltimore, m Theodore Hooper Apr 14 1897 at 10 a.m.
at 1406 Park Avenue p 132

GOODRIDGE Malcolm m Henrietta Tyson Perry on Jun 30 1898 by Reverend William
R. Lord p 132

GORSUCH William Herbert of Baltimore County, m Edna A. Walworth of Baltimore
on Dec 11 1894 at 7 p.m. in the church p 131

GOULD James listed as a comm of the church in 1865 p 78

GOVER Elizabeth Starbuck dau of Henry Taylor and Ann Eliza Gover, b Sep 17
1863, bapt Good Friday, Apr 3 1896 in the church, conf Good Friday Apr 3
1896, joined the church Easter Sunday Apr 5 1896 pp 70-1/2, 87

GOVER Henry Taylor and Ann Eliza Gover p of Elizabeth Starbuck Gover pp70-1/2
and 87

GOVER Miriam b in Waterford, Louden County VA on Dec 12 1855, bapt Jan 7 1894
and received comm, d Mar 8 1920, funeral Mar 10 1920, Reverend C.C.Clark
officiating pp 68, 97

GRAFFLIN, Anne L. m Walter Vrooman on Feb 25 1897 at 10 a.m. (Thursday), at
1123 Saint Paul Street p 132

GRAMMER Catherine m John Stanley on Feb 1 1855 p 115

GRANNISS George F. m Matilda J. Burgess on Nov 1 1866 in Baltimore by John
F.W. Ware p 121

GRAY Sophia S. m Charles A. Vedder on May 5 1908 at 10:30 a.m. at 1314
Bolton Street, Alfred Rodman Hussey officiating (both of Baltimore) p 134

GRAYSON Jane L. m John E. Groome(s) on Dec 9 1851 p 113

GREEN Mary C. m William E. Mayhew on Apr 25 1843p 109

GREEN William m Marie Stuart on Aug 13 1857 p 116

GREENWOOD F.W.P. baptisms by ----- p 11

GREENWOOD F.W.P. marriages by ----- p 103

GRIFFITH Henrietta m William Penniman on Jul 10 1819, both of Baltimore p 101

GRIFFITH Mary Ann m John Hathaway on Mar 15 1821 p 102

GROOME(S) John E. (see also Groome, John E.) m to Jane L. Grayson on Dec 9 1851
p 113

GROSS Rosa L. m Alonzo Lilly in the chapel on Jun 22 1895 p 131

GUILD E. C. baptisms during the ministry of -----; marriages during the
ministry of ----- pp 50, 123

GUILD Edward C. and Emma M. Guild p of Emma Rosalie p 50

GUILD Emma Rosalie dau of Edward C. and Emma M. Guild, bapt Dec 19 1869 at the
home of the Pastor by Reverend L.P. Chamberlain p 50
HALL Ellridge G. m Amanda Bosley on May 19 1858 p 117
HALL Thomas W. m Elizabeth S. Ward on May 22 1832, both of Baltimore p 106
HALLER Alice May dau of Major Granville O. Haller and Henrietta M. Haller, b
Jul 9 1850, bapt Sep 2 1850 p 36
HALLER Major Granville and Henrietta M. Haller p of Alice May p 36
HAMBURGER Samuel m Bessie Emmart on Sep 29 1904 at 5:30 p.m., at 219 W.
Lafayette Avenue, both of Baltimore, Alfred R. Hussey officiating p 134
HAMBURGER Walter S. m Ida Fredericksen on May 22 1905 at 11 a.m. at 219 North
Broadway, Alfred R. Hussey officiating, both of Baltimore p 134
HAMPSON Isabel listed as a comm of the church in Sep 29 1869 p 81
HANDLER Charles conf on Easter Sunday 1900, m Leona E. deMartello on Jan 18
1911 at 7:30 p.m. in the church, Alfred R. Hussey officiating pp 135, 88
HANDLER Charles and Leona De Martello Handler p of Charles Martello p 74,
Leona p 74
HANDLER Charles Martello son of Leona De Martello Handler and Charles Handler,
b Apr 2 1912, bapt Jun 16 1912 in the church p 74
HANDLER Katie conf on May 31 1903, Whitsunday, by Alfred Rodman Hussey p 90
HANDLER Leona dau of Leona De Martello Handler and Charles Handler, b Jun 1915,
bapt Jan 16 1916 in the church p 74
HARRIS George Munroe son of William Callender Harris and Mahitabel Harris,
b May 25 1821, bapt Jun 1 1822 p 8
HARRIS William Callender son of William Callender Harris and Mahitabel Harris,
b May 10 1819, bapt Jun 1 1822 p 8
HARRIS William Callender and Mahitabel Harris p of William Callender and
Mahitabel Harris p of William Callender p 8, George Munroe p 8
HASTINGS Frances Anne dau of John and Mary A. Hastings, bapt Sep 28 1823 p 10
HASTINGS John m Mary A. Sweeting on May 7 1822, both of Baltimore p 102
HASTINGS John and Mary A. p of Frances Anne p 10, William Donalson p 14
HASTINGS Nathan, three of his children were bapt on May 6 1820 p 5
HASTINGS William Donalson son of John Hastings, bapt Oct 1 1828 p 14
HAYLECK Charles R. m Mamie E. Kolb on Nov 26 1919, both of Baltimore p 137
HEALY Penelope I. m Abeather(?) W. Field on Sep 8 1856 p 116
HEIGER Edwin John b Dec 25 1873, conf and joined the church on Nov 6 1892 p 86
HEIM Katie conf and joined the church on Jun 6 1897, Whitsunday p 88
HEIRD Henry W. m to Georgiana B. Cate on Nov 15 1853 p 114
HENERY James son of William and Jan Henery, b Sep 22 1851, bapt Jun 30 1852
p 38
HENERY William and Jan p of James p 38
HENNEBURGER Allan League son of Florence League Henneburger and Elmer
Henneburger, bapt May 30 1915 in the church p 74
HENNEBURGER Elmer m to Florence League on Oct 2 1907 at 4 p.m. in the chapel,
Alfred R. Hussey officiating p 134
HENNEBURGER Elmer and Florence League Henneburger p of Allan League p 74
HENNEBURGER J.R. conf on Easter Sunday 1900 p 88
HEWES Edwin and Martha (Gover) Hewes p of Helen p 68
HEWES Helen dau of Edwin and Martha (Gover) Hewes, b Sep 25 1890, bapt
Mar 25 1894 p 68
HEWSON Bethune Washburn m Emily L. Williams of Baltimore on Nov 2 1830;
Mr. Hewson was from Petersburg, VA p 105
HEWSON Bethune Washburn and Emily L. Hewson p of John Williams p 16
HEWSON John Williams son of Bethune W. and Emily L. Hewson, bapt in Nov 1831
p 16

HICKMAN Alice Louisa dau of Thomas Emerson and Margaret Florence (Squires) Hickman, b Nov 6 1895, bapt Apr 5 1896, Easter, in the church p 70-1/2

HICKMAN Joseph Emerson son of Thomas E. and Mollie (Margaret) Florence (Squires) Hickman, b Oct 6 1897, bapt Jun 2 1898 in the church p 71

HICKMAN Roland Ranstead son of Thomas E. and Mollie F. (Squires) Hickman, b Nov 29 1893, bapt Apr 29 1894 in the church p 69

HICKMAN Thomas E. and Margaret (Mollie) Florence (Squires) Hickman p of Roland Ranstead p 69, Alice Louisa p 70-1/2, Joseph Emerson p 71

HILGENBERG Carl George m Angelica Rogge on Jan 11 1898 at 6 p.m., Tuesday, in the church, both of Baltimore, Albert Walkley officiating p 132

HILKEN Annia Sophie conf on Good Friday Apr 12 1895, joined the church on Easter Sunday Apr 14 1895 p 87

HILKEN Henry Gerhard son of Paul Gerhard Luediger Hilken and Frances Helen (Parsons) Hilken, b Jan 8 1909, bapt Apr 11 1909, Easter Sunday, in the church p 73

HILKEN Paul Gerhard Luediger and Helen Frances (Parsons) Hilken, p of Henry Gerhard p 73, Sarah Parsons p 73

HILKEN Sarah Parsons dau of Paul Gerhard Luediger Hilken and Helen Frances (Parsons) Hilken, b Jun 6 1911, bapt Oct 29 1911 at 512 Woodlawn Road, Roland Park p 73

HILL David of Philadelphia, m Ann Smith of Baltimore on Jun 28 1837 p 108

HILL William m to Mary Jane Murphy on Jan 19 1854 p 114

HILLS George Henry of Falls River MA, m to Lillian Gertrude Jubb, of Baltimore on Mar 27 1907 at 11 a.m., in the church p 134

HOBBY Caroline Maria dau of Mr. and Mrs. Hobby, bap Mar 30 1821 p 6

HOBBY Mary M. m to Henry Lee Livermore on Nov 3 1842, both of Baltimore p 109

HOBBY Mr. and Mrs. p of Caroline Maria p 6

HODGES Charles William son of John W. and Lucy L. Hodges, b Oct 19 1879, bapt Apr 4 1880 in the church p 57

HODGES John W. and Lucy L. Hodges p of Charles William p 57

HOFFMAN Pastor officiated at the funeral of Charles Caspari, b May 31 1850, d Oct 13 1917, buried Oct 15 1917 (during the ministry of Charles A. Wing) p 95

HOFFMAN Thomas C. m to Helen Maria Carter on Apr 13 1841, both of Baltimore p 109

HOLLAND William Condif b Dec 16 1845, d Jan 13 1918, buried Jan 17 1918, Charles A. Wing officiating p 95

HONEMAN Donald Edwin son of Lillian Bernice (League) Honeman and Edwin Kenneth Honeman, b Sep 26 1919, bapt Dec 21 1919 p 75

HONNEMAN Edwin Kenneth and Lillian Bernice (League) Honeman p of Donald Edwin p 75

HOOPER Quney A. m Mary F. Rivera on Dec 28 1856 p 116

HOOPER Theodore m Frances J. Goodenow on Apr 14 1897 at 10 a.m., Wednesday, at 1406 Park Avenue p 132

HOUSTON Mary H. d May 19 1921, funeral May 21 1921, Harry Foster Burns officiating p 98

HOUSTON Sarah E. m William B. Wilkens on Nov 25 1855 p 115

HOWARD John R. m Caroline Jarvis on Jul 28 1827, both of Baltimore, Mr. Everett of Hallowell ME officiating p 104

HOWARD Volney E. m to Catherine Elizabeth Good(?) on Mar 6 1837 in Washington p 107

HOWELL Capt. Rezin G. m Emily D. Ayres, second dau of Major General Ayres, USA, on Feb 6 1884 at the U.S. Barracks, Washington p 127

HUGHES Harry C. conf and joined the church on Palm Sunday Apr 14 1889 p 86
HUNTER Mary A. m to Amos Luke on Dec 26 1893 at 1:45 p.m. in the First
   Independent Christ's Church, both of Washington DC, A.D. Smith Asst p 130
HUNTING Clarence H. m to Josephine A. Lilly on Jan 2 1890, at 213 W.
   Monument Street at 6:00 p.m., both of Baltimore p 129
HUSSEY Alfred Rodman baptisms by, confirmations by, marriages by pp 72,90,
   133, 134, 135
HUSSEY Alfred Rodman and Mary Warner Hussey p of Mary Elizabeth p 72, Emily
   Morgan p 73
HUSSEY Emily Morgan dau of Alfred Rodman Hussey and Mary Warner Hussey, b
   Dec 13 1908, bapt Easter Sunday Apr 11 1909 p 73
HUSSEY Mary Elizabeth dau of Alfred Rodman Hussey and Mary Warner Hussey,
   b Nov 15 1906, bapt Easter Sunday Apr 15 1906 p 72
HYDE Arnold Smith son of Samuel G. Hyde and wife, b Jan 25 1830, bapt Apr 25
   1830 p 15
HYDE Caroline Jarvis dau of Samuel G. and Catherine Hyde, bapt Dec 15 1822,
   m to Henry James on Jun 4 1850 pp 9, 112
HYDE Catherine dau of Samuel and Catherine Hyde, b Feb 1 1832, bapt Apr 20
   1832 p 17
HYDE Miss C. listed as a member of the church in 1865, 1869 pp 78, 81
HYDE Mrs. Cath. listed as a member of the church in 1865, 1869 pp 78, 81
HYDE Clemence T(oby) m to William Henry Keith on Oct 23 1866, dau of Enoch
   and Susan Hyde, b Jan 12 1844, bapt Oct 5 1844 pp 121, 30
HYDE Enoch Jr. m to Susan Elizabeth Hyde of Baltimore on Oct 24 1837; Mr.
   Hyde was from New Orleans p 108
HYDE Enoch Jr. and Susan Hyde p of Sylvester Loomis Fowler p 23, Ida Louisa
   Ratt p 30, Enoch Pratt p 30, Clemence Toby p 30
HYDE Enoch Pratt son of Enoch and Susan Hyde, b Sep 24 1842, bapt Oct 6 1844
   p 30
HYDE Francis son of Mr. and Mrs. Samuel (G.) Hyde, b circa 1828-1829 p 15
HYDE George m to Sarah Ann Clapp of Baltimore on Sep 17 1839; Mr. Hyde was
   from Boston p 108
HYDE Ida Louisa Ratt dau of Enoch and Susan Hyde, b Sep 24 1842, bapt Oct 6
   1844 p 30
HYDE Maria Louisa dau of Samuel and Catherine Hyde, b Sep 22 1818, bapt Jul 9
   1820, m to Enoch Pratt on Aug 1 1837, both of Baltimore pp 5, 108
HYDE Samuel G. and Catherine p of Susan Elizabeth p 5, Maria Louisa p 5,
   William Sparks p 5, Sophia Leopold p 9, Caroline Jarvis p 9, Francis p 15,
   Arnold Smith p 15, Catherine p 17
HYDE Sophia Leopold dau of Samuel G. and Caroline Hyde, bapt on Dec 15 1822,
   also listed as bapt on Feb 13 1825, listed as a comm of the church in 1865,
   1869 pp 9, 13, 78, 81
HYDE Susan Elizabeth dau of Samuel G. and Catherine Hyde, b Feb 2 1817, bapt
   Mar 4 1821, m to Enoch Hyde Jr., of New Orleans, on Oct 24 1837 pp 5, 108
HYDE Sylvester Loomis Fowler son of Enoch and Susan E. Hyde, b Aug 17 1838,
   bapt Oct 25 1838 p 23
HYDE Mrs. Thomas mother of Warren Gould p 24
HYDE Warren Gould son of Mrs. Thomas Hyde, b Sep 8 1833, bapt Dec 25 1839 p 24
HYDE William Sparks son of Samuel G. and Catherine Hyde, b Oct 5 1820, bapt
   Mar 4 1821 p 5
HYNSON John R. m to Frances E. Chamberlain on Sep 6 1832, both of Baltimore
   p 106

JACKSON Charles M. m to Adeline West on Nov 22 1844 p 110

JACKSON Corinne m Arnold B. Johnson of Washington DC, on Nov 25 1908 at
1:00 p.m., at Mount Royal Avenue; Miss Jackson was from Baltimore, Alfred R.
Hussey officiating p 135

JACKSON Harriet C. m to Issac Coale Jr. on Nov 16 1898 at 225 _____ Avenue,
Roland Park, Baltimore County, by Rev. William R. Lord p 133

JACKSON Mary B. conf on Whitsunday, May 15 1910 by Alfred Rodman Hussey p 92

JAEGER Emma Amelia b Jul 28 1902, dau of Louis and Emma Augusta Jaeger, bapt
Nov 16 1902 during the ministry of Alfred Rodman Hussey p 72

JAEGER Emma Augusta (Jones) conf on Good Friday, Apr 12 1895 and joined the
church on Easter Sunday, Apr 14 1895 p 87

JAEGER Louis conf Easter Sunday Apr 13 1884 during the ministry of Charles
Richmond Weld p 85

JAEGER Louis and Emma Augusta (Jones) p of Emma Amelia p 72

JAMES Henry m to Amelia B. Cate on Feb 20 1851 p 113

JANES Caroline J(arvis) Hyde and Henry p of Edward Bartholomew p 47

JANES Edward Bartholomew son of Henry and Caroline J(arvis) James, b Dec 27
1858, bapt Jul 15 1858 p 47

JANES Henry m to Caroline Jarvis Hyde on Jun 4 1850 p 112

JANES Mrs. Ida listed as a comm of the church in Sep 1869 p 81

JANTSCH Ella m to Paul E. Gesiger on Jun 8 1925, both of Baltimore, Rev.
Charles G. Girelius officiating at his residence, entered by F. Raymond
Stutevant p 138

JARVIS Caroline m to John R. Howard on Jul 28 1827 by Mr. Everett of Hallowell
ME, both of Baltimore p 104

JENCKS Eleanor M. conf on Whitsunday May 31 1914 by Alfred Rodman Hussey p 93

JENCKS Elizabeth of Baltimore, m to Harold H. Wrenn of Norfolk VA on Nov 29
1919, Charles A. Wing officiating p 137

JENCKS Elizabeth Cheney conf on Easter Sunday Apr 16 1911, Alfred Rodman
Hussey officiating p 92

JENCKS Francis M. b May 1 1846, d Sep 13 1918, funeral Sep 15 1918, Charles A.
Wing officiating at the interment Oct 15 1918 p 96

JERWALD(?) Bruce K. of Philadelphia, m to Jennie Lucile Thayer of Baltimore
on Oct 28 1914 at 12:00 noon at 1735 Linden Avenue, Alfred Rodman Hussey
officiating p 136

JOHNSON Arnold B. of Washington DC, m Corinne Jackson of Baltimore on Nov 25
1908 at 1:00 p.m., at ------ Mount Royal Avenue, Alfred R. Hussey,
officiating p 135

JOHNSON Nina Roberta dau of William H. and Anna N. Johnson, b Jul 14 1849,
bapt May 15 1859 p 47

JOHNSON Thomas Rinaldo m to Eliza Caswell Rynex on Feb 12 1846 p 110

JOHNSON William H. and Anna N. Johnson p of Nina Roberta. p 47

JOHNSTON Emeline Victoria dau of Emeline and William Johnston, b Oct 6 1834,
bapt Jun 21 1835 p 19

JOHNSTON William and Emeline p of Emeline Victoria p 19

JONES Beatrice Louisa Pinkney dau of Edward Bradley and Anne Shaw (Tiffany)
Jones, b Sep 16 1881, bapt Christmas Day, Dec 25 1881 p 59

JONES Beatrice Louisa Pin(c)kney conf on Good Friday, Apr 12 1895, joined
the church on Easter Sunday Apr 14 p 87

JONES Campbell Pinkney son of Edward Bradley and Anne Shaw (Tiffany) Jones,
b Wednesday Nov 17 1886, bapt Sunday Dec 5 1886 at 1724 North Calvert Street
at 1:30 p.m. p 61

JONES Edward Bradley Jr. son of Edward Bradley and Ann Shaw (Tiffany) Jones,
    b Feb 28 1884, bapt May 25, Sunday, in church, conf on Whitsunday Jun 3
    1906 by Alfred Rodman Hussey pp 60, 91
JONES Edward Bradley and Anne Shaw Tiffany m at the church on Jan 26 1881,
    both of Baltimore, p of Beatrice Louisa Pinkney p 59, Edward Bradley Jr.
    p 60, Campbell Pinkney p 61
JONES Hanson W. of Atlanta GA, m Harriet C. Manning of Ruxton MD, on Sep 17
    1912 at 5:00 p.m., in Ruxton p 136
JONES Isaac D. m to Georgine S. Gelston on Jul 20 1847 p 111
JONES Richard A. m to Emily Pinkney on Mar 28 1831, both of Baltimore p 105
JONES Rev. William S. of Newport RI, officiated at the funeral of Louis F.
    Young, b 1850, d Jun 6 1920, buried Jun 9 1920 (after Charles A. Wing
    resigned as minister and before the arrival of his successor) p 97
JUBB Lillian Gertrude of Baltimore, m George Henry Hills of Fall River MA
    on Mar 27 1907 at 11:00 a.m., in the church p 134
KAAS Emma m to Alfred Pfitsch on Thanksgiving Day in the church, Nov 28 1889
    at 8:00 p.m. p 128
KABERNAGLE Harry L. conf on Whitsunday Jun 3 1906 by Alfred Rodman Hussey p 91
KABERNAGLE Lulu D. conf on Whitsunday Jun 3 1906 by Alfred Rodman Hussey p 91
KAHN Anna C. m in the church to Herbert E. Dixon, both of Hershey PA, on Nov 4
    1911 at 11 a.m., Alfred R. Hussey officiating p 135
KAISS Henry and Annie p of Lina Ada, b Feb 21 1894, bapt Apr 15 1894 in church,
    b(?) in Anne Arundel County p 68
KAISS Lina Ada dau of Henry and Annie Kaiss, b Feb 21 1894 in Anne Arundel
    County(?), bapt Apr 15 1894 in the church p 68
KEIGHLER Anne Checkly dau of William H. and Elizabeth L. Keighler, b Feb 4
    1844, bapt Jun 27 1844 p 29
KEIGHLER Elizabeth Lathrop dau of William H. and Elizabeth Keighler, b Dec 25
    1849, bapt Jul 14 1850 p 35
KEIGHLER Francis Ames son of William H. and Elizabeth Keighler, b May 22 1846,
    bapt Jan 17 1849 p 34
KEIGHLER Henry b Mar 13 1848, son of William H. and Elizabeth Keighler, bapt
    Jan 17 1849 p 34
KEIGHLER John Checkly son of William H. and Elizabeth Keighler, b Jan 16 1842,
    bapt Jun 27 1844 p 29
KEIGHLER Mary Ashburner dau of William H. and Elizabeth L. Keighler, b Aug 11
    1836, bapt Sep 25 1836 p 21
KEIGHLER Samuel Ames son of William H. and Elizabeth Keighler, b Jun 24 1840,
    bapt Jul 19 1840 p 25
KEIGHLER William H. and Elizabeth L. p of Mary Ashburner p 21, John Checkly
    p 29, Anne Checkly p 29, Francis Ames p 34, Henry p 34, Elizabeth Lathrop
    p 35, Samuel Ames p 25
KEIGHLER William M., William, of New York City m Fannie Wallenstein (Jewess)
    of Baltimore on Apr 23 1878 p 126
KEIL Christina conf on Whitsunday May 31 1903 by Alfred Rodman Hussey p 90
KEIL Henry conf on Whitsunday May 31 1903 by Alfred Rodman Hussey p 90
KEITH Alice Clark dau of Edward and Maria (Maynard) Keith, b Apr 23 1870,
    bapt Jan 26 1873 p 52
KEITH Annie May dau of Edward M. and Maria Keith, b Mar 12 1862, bapt Oct 26
    1862 p 48
KEITH Mrs. Bathsheba P. (see also Mrs. B.P.) listed as a comm of the church
    in 1865 and 1869 pp 78, 81

KEITH Charles Henry son of William H. and Clemence T. Keith, b Dec 25 1871,
    bap Dec 25 1871 (lived but 24 hours), during the ministry of E.C.Guild p 50
KEITH Mrs. Clemence T. listed as a comm of the church in Sep 1869 p 81
KEITH E. H. listed as a comm of the church in 1865 p 78
KEITH Edward M. and Maria p of Alice Clark p 52, Annie May p 48
KEITH Edward Martin son of Martin Keith and wife, b Jul 28 1824, bapt Nov 7
    1841 p 26
KEITH Georgianna b Mar 7 1833, bapt Nov 7 1841, dau of Martin Keith and wife
    p 26
KEITH John Alexander son of Martin Keith and wife, b Aug 21 1835, bapt Nov 7
    1841 p 26
KEITH Julia (Miss) listed as a comm of the church in 1865 and 1869 pp 78, 81
KEITH Julia Sparow dau of Martin Keith and wife, b Dec 12 1822(?), bapt Nov 7
    1841 p 26
KEITH Mabel Ida dau of William Henry and Clemence Toby, b Jul 17 1877, bapt
    Jun 2 1878 at 76 Decker Street p 55
KEITH Mrs. Maria M. listed as a comm of the church in Sep 1869 p 81
KEITH Martin and Wife p of Edward Martin p 26, Julia Sparow p 26, Georgianna
    p 26, John Alexander p 26, William Henry p 38
KEITH William H. and Clemence T. p of Charles Henry p 50, Mabel Ida p 55
KEITH William Henry son of Martin Keith and wife, b Dec 23 1841, bapt Jul 16
    1852 p 38
KENNEDY Mary Anne, Mary Anne of Baltimore, m Samuel Phipps of Roxbury MA
    on Sep 27 1840 p 109
KERKER John and Matilda p of John Robert, b Mar 30 1854, bapt Dec 18 1855 p 42
KERKER John Robert son of John and Matilda Kerker, b Mar 30 1854, bapt Dec 18
    1855 p 42
KESLER Katharine Virginia m to Charles L. Stockhausen on Sep 24 1903 at 8:00
    p.m. in the church, both of Baltimore, Alfred R. Hussey officiating p 133
KEY Francis S. m to Beatrice Tiffany on Jun 29 1889 at 10:00 a.m. in the
    church, both of Baltimore p 128
KEYES Caroline Florence m to Edmund Tileston Mudge on Nov 25 1870 at the
    church, during the ministry of E.C.Guild p 123
KEYES George Stuart and Emma C. p of John Brooks Keyes p 59
KEYES John Brooks son of George Stuart and Emma C. Keyes, b Jan 2 1883, bapt
    May 27 1883 in the church p 59
KIDDER Camiltus and Sarah H. p of Elizabeth p 37, Camiltus George p 37
KIDDER Camiltus George son of Camiltus and Sarah H. Kidder, b Jul 6 1850,
    bapt Mar 27 1851 p 37
KIDDER Elizabeth dau of Camiltus and Sarah H. Kidder, b Sep 6 1835(?), bapt
    Mar 27 1851 p 37
KILBOURN Frances J. m to James E. Wollington on Oct 24 1854 p 115
KNOX Adelaide Kilburn dau of William Fay and Sally Ann (Mudge) Knox, b Oct 6
    1877, bapt Feb 13 1879 at 135 Bolton Street p 56
KNOX Catharine Phillips dau of William Fay and Sally Ann (Mudge) Knox, b
    Feb 13 1884, bapt Dec 26 1884 at 135 Bolton Street p 61
KNOX Donald Ross son of William Fay and Sally Ann (Mudge) Knox, b Nov 20
    1888, bapt Feb 3 1891 at 1410 Bolton Street p 65
KNOX John Calvin son of William Fay and Sally Ann (Mudge) Knox, b Sep 12 1886,
    bapt on Feb 3 1891 at 1410 Bolton Street p 65
KNOX William Fay m to Sally Ann Mudge on Feb 12 1873 at 12:00 noon in the
    church, both of Baltimore, during the ministry of C.K.Weld and by him p 125

KNOX William Fay and Sally Ann (Mudge) p of Adelaide Kilburn p 56, Catharine
    Phillips p 61, John Calvin p 65, Donald Ross p 65
KOLB Henrietta Elisabeth conf on Good Friday Apr 12 1895, joined the church
    on Easter Sunday Apr 14 1895 p 87
KOLB Louis conf on Whitsunday May 31 1903, Alfred Rodman Hussey officiating
    p 90
KOLB Louise Amelia conf and joined the church on Jun 6 1897, Whitsunday p 88
KOLB Mamie E. m to Charles R. Hayleck on Nov 26 1919, both of Baltimore p 137
KOLB Matilda J. conf and joined the church on Palm Sunday Apr 14 1889 p 86
KOLB Selma (see also Kolb, Selina) conf and joined the church on Palm Sunday
    Apr 14 1889 p 86
KONIG Louisa Wald (see also Louisa Ward Konig) conf and joined the church on
    Palm Sunday Apr 14 1889 p 86
KRABER Daniel m to Emily Bines, both of Baltimore, on Apr 23 1833 p 107
KRAUSSE Henrietta (see also Krause, Henrietta) conf during the ministry of
    Charles Richmond Weld on Jun 8 1878 p 85
KRAUTER William conf on Whitsunday May 31 1903 by Alfred Rodman Hussey p 90
KUHN Kate of Baltimore, m to David Zenker of Kent County on Nov 3 1886, in
    the church at 7:00 p.m. p 127
LAMPHER Charlotte Alice dau of Regina P. Lampher and Raymond W. Lampher,
    b Sep 24 1911, bapt Easter Sunday Apr 7 1912 in the church p 74
LAMPHER Raymond W. m to Regina P. Sauer, both of Baltimore, on Apr 30 1907
    at 4:00 p.m., in the building at 1314 Bolton Street, Alfred R. Hussey
    officiating p 134
LAMPHER Raymond W. and Regina P. p of Charlotte Alice p 74
LANAGAN Effie (see also Lanagin, Edith) dau of Michael J. and Anna L. Lanagan,
    b in Memphis TN on Oct 15 1866, bapt Jun 1 1879, Whitsunday, in the church
    p 56
LANAGAN Michael J. and Anna L. (see also Lanagin, Michael J. and Anna L.) p of
    Effie (see also Edith) p 56
LANGREN Josephine G. of Baltimore, m to Frank W. Bull of Pittsburg PA on
    Feb 22 1877 at the church p 125
LANGREW (Lungrew?) Josephine Griswold of Toledo OH, m to Frank Webster Ball
    of Grand Rapids MI on Feb 22 1877 at the church p 126
LANSALD Miranda (see also Lansdale, Miranda) m to Alexander Miller on Mar 21
    1848 p 112
LAUER Augusta Frederica conf and joined the church, conf on Good Friday Apr 12
    1895, joined the church on Easter Sunday Apr 14 1895 p 87
LEA William Jr. m to Sarah B. Bently of Montgomery County MD on Jun 20 1867
    by John F.W. Ware p 122
LEAGUE Arthur B. and Emma Lillian (McDonald) p of Lillian Bernice p 73, Arthur
    Ellsworth p 73, Maria Elizabeth p 73, Mildred Frances p 73
LEAGUE Arthur Burchhead b Mar 20 1882, bapt Easter Sunday Mar 27 1910 in the
    church, during the ministry of Alfred Rodman Hussey p 73
LEAGUE Arthur Ellsworth son of Arthur B. League and Emma Lillian (McDonald)
    League, b Jun 22 1902, bapt Easter Sunday Mar 27 1910 during the ministry
    of Alfred Rodman Hussey p 73
LEAGUE Elmer Ellsworth son of Martin and Louisa League, b Aug 25 1891, bapt
    Apr 28 1893 in the chapel by Revd. Charles T. Sempers p 66
LEAGUE Florence dau of Martin and Louisa League, b Sep 22 1889, bapt Apr 28
    1893 in the chapel by Revd. Charles T. Sempers, conf on Jun 11 1905,
    Whitsunday, by Alfred Rodman Hussey p 91

LEAGUE Florence m to Elmer Henneburger (see also Henneberger, Elmer) on
    Oct 2 1907 at 4:00 p.m., in the chapel, both of Baltimore, Alfred R.
    Hussey officiating p 134
LEAGUE Howard H. m to Elizabeth Rudoeph (see also Elizabeth Rudolph) on
    Nov 17 1893 at 8:00 p.m.,in the chapel p 130
LEAGUE Lillian Bernice dau of Arthur B. League and Emma Lillian (McDonald)
    League, b May 17 1900, bapt Mar 27 1910, Easter Sunday, in the church,
    Alfred Rodman Hussey officiating p 73
LEAGUE Maria Elizabeth dau of Arthur B. League and Emma Lillian (McDonald)
    League, b Sep 27 1901, bapt Mar 27 1910, Easter Sunday, during the
    ministry of Alfred Rodman Hussey p 73
LEAGUE Martin and Louisa p of Florence p 66, Elmer Ellsworth p 66
LEAGUE Mildred Frances dau of Arthur B. League and Emma Lillian (McDonald)
    League, b Aug 16 1905, bapt Easter Sunday Mar 27 1910, during the
    ministry of Alfred Rodman Hussey p 73
LEAGUE Stella conf by Alfred R. Hussey on May 31 1903, Whitsunday p 90
LEARNY Jeannie m to William Cathcart Day, Ph.D. on Dec 27 1884 in the church
    at 5:30 p.m., both of Baltimore p 127
LEAVERTON Estella conf on Whitsunday May 22 1904 by Alfred Rodman Hussey p 90
LEE Roberta m to Joseph C. France of Baltimore on Sep 24 1892 at 11:15 a.m.,
    in the chapel, dau of Adolphe and Margaret (Torney) Simon of Baltimore p 130
LEMMON Clara Virginia conf on Good Friday Apr 12 1895, joined the church on
    Easter Sunday Apr 14 1895 p 87
LEWIS Fanny Broom dau of John Toy(?) and Anne Rebecca Lewis, b Jun 22 1856,
    bapt Jul 10 1857 p 45
LEWIS John Toy(?) and Anne Rebecca p of Fanny Broom p 45
LEWIS Warren H. of Baltimore m to Margaret A. Reed of New York on May 23 at
    3:00 p.m., at Cedar Lawn, Govans MD, Alfred Rodman Hussey officiating p 135
LILLY A. Jr. listed as a member of the church in 1865 p 78
LILLY Albert son of Alonzo and Mary Ann Lilly, b Dec 12 1841, bapt Jun 7
    1843 p 28
LILLY Alonzo listed as a comm of the church in Sep 1869 p 81
LILLY Alonzo son of Alonzo Lilly Jr. and Kate Ludlow Lilly, bapt Jun 19 1872
    at the home of Mr. Mowinkel during the ministry of E.C. Guild p 50
LILLY Alonzo m to Rosa L. Gross on Jun 22 1895 in the church's chapel p 131
LILLY Alonzo Jr. and Ann Catherine W(ethered) Ludlow p of Alonzo p 50, Ludlow
    p 53, Channing p 56, Wethered Ludlow p 60, Josephine Augusta p 48
LILLY Alonzo and Wife (possibly Mary Ann) p of Lavinia (see also Laence) p 25,
    Lewis p 16, Charles p 22, Diana p 25*, Alonzo p 25, Albert p 28, Channing
    p 31, *possibly Oriana
LILLY Channing son of Alonzo Lilly and Wife, b Dec 21 1844, bapt Nov 11 1845
    p 31
LILLY Channing Francis son of Alonzo Lilly Jr. and Ann Catherine W(ethered)
    Ludlow, b Aug 28 1878, bapt May 4 1879 at 95 W. Monument Street p 56
LILLY ChanningFrancis son of Channing Francis Lilly and Gertrude (Bosee)(?)
    Lilly, b Sep 10 1906, bapt Mar 3 1907 p 73
LILLY Charles son of Alonzo Lilly and Wife, b Mar 25 1832, bapt Dec 20 1837
    p 22
LILLY Diana (possibly Oriana) dau of Alonzo Lilly and Wife, b Jun 23 1838,
    bapt Nov 8 1840 p 25
LILLY Diana (possibly Oriana) listed as comm of the church in Sep 1869 p 81
LILLY Emilina dau of Alonzo Lilly and Wife, b Jul 16 1835, bapt Nov 8 1840
    p 25

LILLY Emma m to John J. Thomsen on Oct 10 1852 p 114

LILLY Josephine A(ugusta) dau of Alonzo Lilly Jr., bapt in Nov 1865, m to
    Clarence H. Hunting at 6:00 p.m., Jan 2 1890 at 213 W. Monument Street,
    both of Baltimore pp 48, 129

LILLY Kate L. (Mrs.) listed as a comm of the church on Jan 1 1871 p 82

LILLY Lavinia (see also Laence) m to Preston Ware on Jun 16 1846 p 111

LILLY Lewis son of Alonzo Lilly and Wife, bapt Jun 21 1831 p 16

LILLY Ludlow son of Alonzo Jr. and Ann Catherine W(ethered) Ludlow Lilly,
    bapt May 16 1875, Whitsunday, in the church, b May 27 1874, d Jan 14 1921,
    funeral Jan 18 1921, Rev. Joseph Henry Crooker, D.D. officiating pp 53, 97

LILLY Mary Ann (Mrs.) listed as a comm of the church in Sep 1869 (possibly
    Mrs. Alonzo Lilly) p 81

LILLY N. listed as a member of the church in 1865 p 78

LILLY Wethered Ludlow son of Alonzo Lilly Jr. and Ann Catherine Wethered
    (Ludlow) Lilly, b Jun 21 1883, bapt Jan 1 1884 p 60

LILLY William D. conf on Whitsunday May 31 1903 by Alfred Rodman Hussey p 90

LIPPINCOTT Samuel W. bapt Apr 6 1890 in the church p 64

LIVERRMORE Henry Lee m to Mary M. Hobby on Nov 3 1842, both of Baltimore p 109

LLOYD William G. m to Adeline Bishop on Jan 15 1852 p 114

LORD Daniel S. m to Theresa H. Menden on Jul 16 1854 p 114

LORD William R. Rev. officiated at the wedding of Isaac Coule Jr. and
    Harriet C. Jackson, on Nov 16 1898 at 225 -------Avenue, Roland Park,
    Baltimore County p 133

LOWRY R.K. Mr. father of James Lowry Donaldson and Robert Oliver, both
    children bapt on May 12, Sunday, 1819 p 3

LUCKE Ida Blanche conf on Whitsunday May 19 1907 by Alfred Rodman Hussey,
    m to William H. Wilbur on Jun 10 1911 at 3:00 p.m., at 3605 Windsor Mill
    Road, Walbrook, Alfred Rodman Hussey officiating pp 91, 135

LUCKE Katherine C. conf on May 22 1904, Whitsunday, by Alfred Rodman Hussey
    p 90

LUKE Amos m Mary A. Hunter on Dec 26 1893 at 1:45 p.m., both of Washington DC,
    A.D. Smith, Asst. officiating p 130

MC CAWLEY Robert H. of Hagerstown PA(?) m Edna Pfifferkorn of Baltimore on
    Sep 18 1912 in the church, Alfred Rodman Hussey officiating p 136

MC CORKLE Harry A. of Baltimore m Claudia K. Orris of Johnstown PA on Apr 16
    1910 at 6:30 p.m., at 1314 Bolton Street, Alfred Rodman Hussey officiating
    p 135

MC COY Charles Leonard son of Charles W. and Lucretia McCoy, b Jan 30 1857,
    bapt Apr 9 1857 p 44

MC COY Charles W. C. m to Lucretia V(ashti) Bartlett on May 3 1854, p of
    George Bartlett p 42, Charles Leonard p 44, p 114

MC COY George Bartlett son of Charles W.C. McCoy and Lucretia V(ashti) McCoy,
    b Mar 17 1855, bapt Jun 12 1855 p 42

MC COY Louis Bartlett son of Louis McAtee McCoy and Augusta Malvena (Wicks)
    McCoy, b Aug 11 1892, bapt Oct 18 1892 at 10:30 a.m., in the chapel p 66

MC COY Louis McAtee and Augusta Malvena (Wicks) McCoy p of Louis Bartlett
    McCoy p 66

MC DERMOT Isabella m to Hartford Sweet on Nov 6 1849 p 112

MC DONALD Emma Lillian, dau of George Ellsworth and Mary Lizzie (Welch)
    McDonald, b Mar 20 1882, bapt Mar 27 1910, Easter Sunday, in church, wife
    of Arthur Burchhead League p 73

MC DONALD George Ellsworth and Mary Lizzie Welch McDonald p of Mollie Gertrude
    p 73, Emma Lillian p 73

MC DONALD Mollie Gertrude dau of George Ellsworth and Mary Lizzie (Welch) McDonald, b Jul 27 1884, bapt Mar 27 1910, Easter Sunday, in church p 73

MC DOWELL E. G. listed as a comm of the church in 1865 p 79

MC DOWELL Edward Goodwin son of Robert and Susan G. McDowell, b Jul 15 1837, bapt May 20 1838 p 23

MC DOWELL H. M. Miss listed as a comm of the church in 1865 p 78

MC DOWELL Robert and Susan G. p of Edward Goodwin p 23

MC FARLAND Cephas Dodd m Emily W. Chubb in Washington DC on Nov 2 1865, both of Baltimore, John F.W. Ware officiating p 121

MC FARLAND Emily Mrs. listed as a comm of the church in Sep 1869 p 81

MC GINN Margaret R. m to John R. Cole on Mar 31 1835, both of Baltimore p 107

MC GINN Martha m to Washington March on May 25 1837, both of Baltimore p 108

MC GOWAN Matilda J. m to Joshua Burgess on Oct 4 1853 p 114

MC KEENE Caroline dau of Isaac and Mary McKeene, b Mar 9 1842, bapt Oct 9 1842 p 27

MC KEENE Isaac and Mary p of Caroline p 27

MC KEEVER Isaac father of James Laurence p 22, Marion Sanford p 22

MC KEEVER James Laurence son of Isaac McKeever, b Oct 4 1831, bapt Jun 11 1837 p 22

MC KEEVER Marion Sanford child of Isaac McKeever, b Nov 23 1835, bapt Jun 11 1837 p 22

MC KENTHUM Hannah Columbia b at sea on May 22 1867, bapt Apr 1 1888, Easter Sunday, in the church p 63

MC KENZIE George N. and Martha p of George Norbury p 43, Harry Downing p 43, Lillie p 43

MC KENZIE George Norbury son of George N. and Martha McKenzie, b May 4 1851, bapt Apr 26 1856 p 43

MC KENZIE Harry Downing son of George N. and Martha McKenzie, b Oct 25 1854, bapt Apr 26 1856 p 43

MC KENZIE Lillie dau of George N. and Martha McKenzie, b May 30 1855, bapt Apr 26 1856 p 43

MC NULTY Mary m to William A. Purdy on Oct 17 1850 p 113

MC PHERSON Clara P. conf on Jun 11 1905, Whitsunday, by Alfred Rodman Hussey p 91

MACKAY Robert and Emma p of Thomas Carlyle p 64

MACKAY Thomas Carlyle son of Robert and Emma Carlyle, b Jun 17 1888, bapt Jun 16 1889 p 64

MAHANEY Rebecca m to William Reteu on May 13 1819, both of Baltimore p 101

MAIDLOW Charles son of Charles C. and Sarah Maidlow, b Jan 30 1855, bapt Sep 20 1857 p 45

MAIDLOW Charles C. and Sarah p of Mary Whittimor p 39, Isabel p 39, James p 39, Charles p 45, Kate p 45

MAIDLOW Isabel dau of Charles C. and Sarah Maidlow, b Jan 25 1849, bapt May 29 1853 p 39

MAIDLOW James son of Charles C. and Sarah Maidlow, b Sep 4 1852, bapt May 29 1853 p 39

MAIDLOW Kate dau of Charles C. and Sarah Maidlow, b Mar 6 1857, bapt Sep 20 1857 p 45

MAIDLOW Mary Elizabeth bapt on May 29 1853 (adult) p 39

MAIDLOW Mary Whittemor dau of Charles C. and Sarah Maidlow, b Jun 5 1836, bapt May 29 1853 p 39

MANNING Amy Russell dau of Cleveland Pratt and Arabella Russell Manning, b in Baltimore on Jan 14 1893, bapt May 23 1893 p 67

MANNING Charles Bartlett son of Charles Henry and Fanny Bartlett Manning, b
Aug 5 1873, bapt on Thanksgiving Day Nov 24 1881 in the church p 58
MANNING Charles Henry and Fanny Bartlett p of Robert Livermore p 58, Charles
Bartlett, p 58
MANNING Cleveland and Arabella Russell Manning p of Amy Russell, b 1893 p 67
MANNING Cleveland Pratt son of Joseph C. and Rebecca Manning, b May 28 1854,
bapt Sep 14 1856, m to Arabella Russell on Jun 5 1888 at 12:00 noon in the
church, both of Baltimore pp 43, 128
MANNING Dorothy Cogswell dau of Joseph C. and Laura R. (Darley) Manning, b
May 7 1884, bapt Oct 9 1887 p 62
MANNING Edith Livermore dau of Joseph C. and Laura R. (Darley) Manning, b
Apr 11 1879, bapt Jun 1 1879, Whitsunday, in the church p 56
MANNING Frances Bartlett dau of Joseph C. and Laura R. (Darley) Manning, b
Dec 5 1885, bapt Oct 9 1887 at Lake Roland, conf on Whitsunday, May 30
1909 by Alfred Rodman Hussey p 63
MANNING Harriet Cleveland dau of Joseph C. and Laura (Darley) Manning, b
Jun 11 1881, bapt Nov 24 1881, Thanksgiving Day, at the church, conf and
joined the church on Jun 6, Whitsunday 1897 pp 58, 88
MANNING Harriet Cleveland m on Sep 17 1912 at 5:00 p.m., in Ruxton MD to
Hanson W. Jones of Atlanta GA, Alfred R. Hussey officiating p 136
MANNING Henry Livermore son of Joseph C. and Rebecca Manning, b Jan 11 1852,
bapt Apr 11 1852 p 38
MANNING James Buchanan son of Samuel and Susan Manning, b Sep 25 1835, bapt
Oct 25 1835 p 20
MANNING Joseph C. and Laura R. Darley m on Jan 6 1874 in Baltimore at the
church at 1:00 p.m., both of Baltimore p 125
MANNING Joseph C. and Laura R. Darley, p of Mary Darley, b 1875 p 53, Edith
Livermore, b 1879 p 56, Harriet Cleveland, b 1881 p 58, Dorothy Cogswell,
b 1884 p 62, Frances Bartlett, b 1885 p 63, Joseph Cogswell, b 1887 p 64,
Clara Fish, b 1889 p 53
MANNING Joseph C. and Rebecca p of Mary Elizabeth, b 1842 p 27, Joseph Cogswell
b 1847 p 33, Rebecca Livermore, b 1849 p 35, Henry Livermore, b 1853 p 38,
Cleveland Pratt, b 1854 p 43, Leonard Jarvis, b 1856 p 43
MANNING Joseph Cogswell son of Joseph C. and Rebecca Manning, b Jun 1847, bapt
Jan 23 1848, listed as a comm of the church in Jan 1872 pp 33, 82
MANNING Joseph Cogswell son of Joseph Cogswell and Laura Rebecca Manning, b
Nov 17 1887, bapt Nov 7 1889 at 1919 Park Avenue, conf on Whitsunday May 19
1907 by Alfred Rodman Hussey pp 64, 91
MANNING Laura Rebecca b Nov 11 1849, d Oct 28 1919, funeral Oct 31 1919, Alfred
R. Hussey and Charles A. Wing officiating p 96
MANNING Leonard Jarvis son of Joseph C. and Rebecca Manning, b May 11 1856,
bapt Sep 14 1856 p 43
MANNING Lucy Ann dau of Samuel and Susan Manning, b Jun 14 1831, bapt Oct 25
1835 p 20
MANNING Mary Darley dau of Joseph C. and Laura R. (Darley) Manning, b Feb 3
1875, bapt May 16 1875, Whitsunday, in the church, conf on Good Friday
Apr 12 1895, joined the church Easter Sunday Apr 14 1895 pp 53, 87
MANNING Mary Elizabeth dau of Joseph and Rebecca P.J. Manning, b Aug 25 1842,
bapt Jan 21 1843 p 27
MANNING Rebecca Livermore (see also Manning, Rebecca Levering) dau of Joseph
C. and Rebecca Manning, b Aug 8 1849, bapt Feb 3 1850 p 35
MANNING Robert Livermore son of Charles Henry and Fanny Bartlett Manning,
b Aug 5 1873, bapt Nov 24 1881, Thanksgiving Day, in the church p 58

MANNING Samuel son of Samuel and Susan Manning, b Mar 15 1832, bapt Oct 25
    1835 p 20

MANNING Samuel and Susan p of Lucy Ann p 20, Samuel p 20, William Sheppard
    p 20, James Buchanan p 20

MANNING William Sheppard son of Samuel and Susan Manning, b Jan 12 1834, bapt
    Oct 25 1835 p 20

MARCH Washington m to Martha McGinn on May 25 1837, both of Baltimore p 108

MAREDITH Charles V(ivian) and Sophie Gooding (Rose Maredith (see also
    Merridth, Charles V. and Meredith, Charles V.) p of Kate Rose p 55, Sophie
    Rose p 58, Sarah Bernard p 59

MAREDITH Kate Rose dau of Charles Vivian and Sophie Gooding (Rose) Maredith,
    b Apr 23 1878, bapt Jun 9 1878, Whitsunday, at 412 Eutaw Street p 55

MAREDITH Sarah Bernard dau of Charles V(ivian) and Sophie Gooding (Rose)
    Maredith of Richmond VA, b Dec 24 1882, bapt Jun 20 1883 at Ridge Lawn,
    Baltimore County MD p 59

MAREDITH Sophie Rose (see also Merridith) dau of Charles V. and Sophie Godding
    (Rose) Maredith, of Richmond VA, b in Baltimore Dec 5 1880, bapt Mar 6 1881
    in the church p 58

MAROBELL Henry m to Mary Atcheson on Jun 28 1855 p 115

MARSHALL John conf on Easter Sunday 1900 p 88

MARSTON Martha m to William Tileston on Oct 11 1832 p 106

MARTELLO Leona conf on May 31 1903, Whitsunday, by Alfred Rodman Hussey p 90

MARTIN Eva R. m to James A. Miller on Dec 24 1866, both of Baltimore p 122

MARTIN Thomley W. of New York, m Hulda R. Rohr of Baltimore on Oct 5 1904
    at 12 noon, Alfred Rodman Hussey officiating p 134

MASON Luther W. m to Hannah E. Allen on Oct 16 1845 p 111

MAYER Alfred Marshall son of Charles F. and Eliza C. Mayer, b Nov 13 1836,
    bapt Apr 18 1837 p 22

MAYER Ann Catharine dau of Charles F. and Eliza Mayer, bapt Jan 1 1830 p 15

MAYER Anna Maria dau of Brantz and Mary Mayer, b Apr 1841, bapt Dec 21 1845
    p 31

MAYER Brantz m to Cornelia Poor on Nov 15 1848 p 112

MAYER Brantz and Cornelia p of Cornelia p 35, Jane p 38

MAYER Brantz and Mary p of Anna Maria p 31, Dora p 31, Mary p 31

MAYER Mrs. B. listed as a comm of the church 1865 p 79

MAYER Charles F. and Eliza C. p of Francis Blackwell p 15, Ann Catherine p 15,
    Charles Frederick p 22, Alfred Marshall p 22, Eliza p 30, Lewis p 22

MAYER Charles Frederick son of Charles F. and Eliza C. Mayer, b Jan 12 1832,
    bapt Apr 18 1837 p 22

MAYER Cornelia dau of Brantz and Cornelia Mayer, b Sep 6 1849, bapt Dec 24
    1849 p 35

MAYER Dora dau of Brantz and Mary Mayer, b Feb 1 1844, bapt Dec 21 1845 p 31

MAYER Eliza dau of Charles F. and Eliza C. Mayer, b Jul 8 1844, bapt Sep 22
    1844 p 30

MAYER Francis Blackwell son of Charles F. and Eliza Mayer, bapt Jan 1 1830
    p 15

MAYER Jane dau of Brantz and Cornelia Mayer, b Feb 27 1851, bapt Dec 24 1851
    p 38

MAYER Jane m to Thomas Kell Bradford on Jun 14 1883 at 16 McCullough Street
    by Rev. Rush R. Shippen, of Washington p 127

MAYER Lewis son of Charles F. and Eliza C. Mayer, b Sep 16 1833, bapt Apr 18
    1837 p 22

MAYER Mary dau of Brantz and Mary Mayer, b Oct 14 1845, bapt Dec 21 1845 p 31

MAYHEW A. E. Mrs. listed as a comm of the church in 1865 p 78

MAYHEW F. L. Mrs. listed as a comm of the church in 1865 p 78

MAYHEW Frances J. Mrs. listed as a comm of the church in 1869 p 81

MAYHEW Susan Brimmer dau of William E. and Maria M. Mayhew bapt on Apr 12 1825 p 13

MAYHEW William E. m to Mary C. Green on Apr 25 1843 (Mary Cogswell Green?) p 109

MAYHEW William E. m to Abby E. Poor on Dec 3 1856 p 116

MAYHEW William E. m to Frances J. Poor on Jun 10 1844 p 110

MAYHEW William E. and Maria M. p of Susan Brimmer, b in 1825 p 13

MAYNARD Susan G. m to William Russell on Dec 24 1845 p 111

MEHRLING Daniel m to Mary Van Burghen on Sep 24 1891 at 4 p.m. in the church, both of Washington p 129

MENDEN Theresa H. m to Daniel S. Lord on Jul 16 1854 p 114

MENNEN Rena of Baltimore, m to Maria L. Van Hoof of Antwerp, Belgium on Oct 29 1921 p 138

MEREDITH Elizabeth Loring dau of Joseph and Mary Meredith, b Feb 20 1855, bapt Apr 13 1855 p 42

MEREDITH Harry son of Joseph and Mary Meredith, b Dec 15(13?) 1849, bapt Apr 4 1850 p 35

MEREDITH J(oseph) H. listed as a comm of the church in 1865 and in 1869 pp 78, 81

MEREDITH Joseph (H.) and Mary p of Mary Gainsworth p 34, Harry p 35, Elizabeth Loring p 42

MEREDITH Mary Mrs. listed as a comm of the church in Sep 1869 p 81

MEREDITH Mary Gainsworth dau of Joseph and Mary Meredith, b Oct 10 1848, bapt Nov 26 1848 p 34

MERRIDITH Charles V. (see also Maredith) of Richmond VA, m to Sophie G. Rose, of Baltimore County on Apr 26 1877 at the home of Col. J.M. Orem, Baltimore County at 12:30 p.m. p 125

MERRIFIELD Edwin m to Sarah E. Coy on Jun 25 1866 by Rev. John F.W. Ware p 121

MERRYMAN Fannie m to George Sterns on Jun 28 1866 in Baltimore by Rev. John F.W. Ware p 121

MEYER Rosa Lee conf and joined the church on Jan 2 1901 p 88

MICKLE Sally m to William Miles on Sep 10 1823 (of Baltimore) p 103

MILES William m to Sally Mickle of Baltimore on Sep 10 1823 p 103

MILLER Alexander m to Miranda Lansald (see also Lansdale) on Mar 21 1848 p 112

MILLER Beulah M. m to Herbert M. Dickinson on Jun 5 1893 at noon in the chapel p 130

MILLER James A. m to Eva R. Martin on Dec 24 1866, both of Baltimore, Rev. John F.W. Ware presiding p 122

MILLS Lillian Viola b in Baltimore Sep 19 1862, conf and joined the church on Whitsunday May 25 1890, m to Albert J. Gminder on Jul 7 at 9:30 a.m. in the church, both of Baltimore 1890 pp 86, 129

MILTENBERGER George W. m to Sarah E. Williams on May 2 1850 p 112

MITCHELL M. P. p of Theodore Edward p 10

MITCHELL Theodore Edward son of M.P. Mitchell, bapt on Sep 28 1823 p 10

MOLINARD Ann M. Mrs. listed as a comm of the church in Sep 1869 p 81

MOLINARD Julian Robinson son of Julian and ------Molinard, bapt Feb 11 1866 p 48

MOLINARD Mrs. listed as a comm of the church in 1865 p 79

MOORE Adelaide Macallister dau of Nettie and William James Moore, b Jan 5 1908, bapt Jun 9 1908 p 73

MOORE Benjamin P. and Florence (Sparks) Moore p of Jared Sparks Moore p 57
MOORE Jared Sparks son of Benjamin P. and Florence (Sparks) Moore, grandson
    of the first pastor of this church, b Sep 29 1879, bapt Mar 22 1880 at
    437 N. Calvert Street p 57
MOORE John Leverett m to Nancy Clark Williams of Baltimore on Dec 23 1891
    at 915 McCulloh Street at 7:30 p.m.; Mr. Moore was from Orange NJ p 129
MOORE John Leverett (Levarett?) and Nancy (Williams) p of Nancy Campbell p 67
MOORE Mary Ann m to John J. Brown on Sep 15 1845 p 110
MOORE Nancy Campbell dau of Nancy (Williams) and John Leverett (Levarett?)
    Moore, b at Vassar College, Poughkeepsie NY on May 13 1893, bapt in the
    church on Dec 31 1893 p 67
MOORE Nettie conf on Easter Sunday 1900 p 88
MOORE William James son of Nettie and William James Moore, b Oct 2 1905, bapt
    Apr 4 1906, during the ministry of Alfred Rodman Hussey p 72
MOORE William James and Nettie p of William James p 72, Adelaide Macallister
    p 73
MORELEY Thomas A. E. m to Rose M. Whitney on May 22 1913 at 8:00 p.m. in the
    church, both of Batlimore, Alfred Rodman Hussey officiating p 136
MORISON Alice Sydney dau of Nathaniel H. and Sydney B. Morison, b Jan 24 1859,
    bapt Jun 10 1859 p 47
MORISON Earnest Nathaniel son of Nathaniel H. and Sydney B. Morison, b Nov 14
    1848, bapt Feb 24 1849 p 34
MORISON Francis son of Nathaniel H. and Sydney B. Morrison, b Mar 18 1844,
    bapt Jun 10 1844 p 29
MORISON George Brown son of Nathaniel H. and Sydney B. Morison, b Jan 5 1846,
    bapt Jun 2 1846 p 32
MORISON John Homes son of Nathaniel H. and Sydney B. Morison, b Jan 24 1857,
    bapt Mar 28 1857 p 44
MORISON N.H. listed as a comm of the church in 1865 and in 1869 pp 78, 81
MORISON Nathaniel H. m to Sydney B. Brown on Dec 17 1842 p 109
MORISON Nathaniel H. and Sydney B. p of Francis p 29, George Brown p 32,
    Earnest Nathaniel p 34, Robert George p 37, John Homes p 44, William
    George p 40, Alice Sydney p 47
MORISON Robert George son of Nathaniel H. and Sidney B. Morison, b Jan 13
    1851, bapt Jul 13 1851 p 37
MORISON Sydney B. Mrs. listed as a comm of the church in Sep 1869 p 81
MORISON William George son of Nathaniel H. and Sydney B. Morison, bapt
    Feb 14 1854 p 40
MORONG Edward P. and Jane S. p of Walter Welsh p 46
MORONG Walter Welsh son of Edward P. and Jane S. Morong, b Apr 6 1858, bapt
    Sep 20 1858 p 46
MORRIS Evelyn Scott conf on Good Friday Apr 3 1896, joined the church on
    Easter Sunday Apr 5 1896 p 87
MORRIS Josephine Cushing dau of Thomas J. and Sally (Cushing) Morris, bapt
    Jun 3 1877 at 132 Park Avenue (listed in the 1922 index as Josephus Cushing
    Morris) p 54
MORRIS Thomas J. and Sally (Cushing) Morris p of Josephine Cushing Morris p 54
MORRIS William U. m to Delia A. Coon on Nov 28 1847 p 112
MORRISON Elizabeth Whittridge dau of Horace and Mary Elizabeth Morrison, b
    Dec 8 1842, bapt May 7 1843 p 28
MORRISON Horace and Mary Elizabeth p of Elizabeth Whittridge p 28, Mary Anne
    p 31, Samuel Lord p 38
MORRISON Mary Anne dau of Horace and Mary Morrison, b Nov 23 1844, bapt
    May 25 1845 p 31

MORRISON Samuel Lord son of Horace and Mary E. Morrison, b Oct 28 1851, bapt
Jun 12 1852 p 38

MORTON Henry m to Mary H. Bryant of Baltimore on Dec 28 1820 p 101

MOTT Richard m to Louisa H. Foyer on Mar 1 1831, both of Baltimore p 105

MOWINKEL Mr., Alonzo Lilly was bapt at his home on June 19 1872, the son of
Alonzo Lilly Jr. and Kate Ludlow Lilly p 50

MUDGE Abner B. m to Catherine C. Phillips on Apr 26 1843 p 110

MUDGE Abner B. and Catherine C. p of Edmund Tileston p 30, Catherine Phillips
p 32, Sally Ann p 33, Henry p 35, Jane p 40, George p 40, Mary Sweeting
p 42, Frank p 47, George Burnap p 48(?)

MUDGE Arthur Phillips son of E. Tiliston and Caroline Florence Howard (Keyes)
both of Pikesville, Baltimore County, Apr 2 1882, bapt Feb 3 1891 at 1410
Bolton Street at 4:30 p.m. Tuesday p 65

MUDGE Catherine Phillips dau of Abner B. and Catherine C. Mudge, b Mar 15
1846, bapt Apr 26 1846 p 32

MUDGE Dorothy Sweeting dau of Frank and Margaret Louise (Simon) Mudge, b Jun
28 1890, bapt Dec 28 1890 in the church p 65

MUDGE Dorothy Sweeting conf on Easter Sunday Apr 16 1911 by Alfred Rodman
Hussey p 92

MUDGE Dorothy Sweeting m to Grove Parker Dean Jr. on May 29 1915 at 12 noon,
at 1752 Park Avenue, Alfred Rodman Hussey officiating p 136

MUDGE E. Tileston and Caroline Florence Howard (Keyes) p of Arthur Phillips
p 65

MUDGE Edmund Tileston son of Abner B. and Catherine C. Mudge, b Sep 13 1844,
bapt Nov 24 1844 p 30

MUDGE Frank son of Abner B. and Catherine C. Mudge, b Oct 23 1858, bapt Jun
12 1859 p 47

MUDGE Frank and Margaret Louise (Simon) p of Margaret Torney p 63, Dorothy
Sweeting p 65, Priscilla Phillips p 66, Louis Goldthwait p 68, Edmund
Tileston p 70

MUDGE George son of Abner B. and Catherine C. Mudge, b Apr 7 1853, bapt
Sep 25 1853 p 40

MUDGE George Burnap bapt by N.H. Chamberlain on Apr 15 1860, b Mar 4 1860,
(possibly the son of Abner B. and Catherine C. Mudge) see Maryland Census
1860, Baltimore City, twentieth ward, p 256, #1822(?), 1825 p 48

MUDGE Jane dau of Abner B. and Catherine C. Mudge, b Sep 6 1851, bapt Sep 25
1853 p 40

MUDGE Louis Goldthwait son of Frank and Margaret Louise (Simon) Mudge, b
Jul 1893, bapt Mar 18 1894, Palm Sunday, in the church p 68

MUDGE Margaret Torney dau of Frank and Margaret Louise (Simon) Mudge, b
Mar 15 1889, bapt Jun 9 1889, Whitsunday, in the church p 63

MUDGE Mary Sweeting dau of Abner B. and Catherine C. Mudge, b Sep 9 1854,
bapt May 27 1855 p 42

MUDGE Priscilla Phillips dau of Frank and Margaret Louise (Simon) Mudge,
b Sep 14 1891, bapt Apr 17 1891, Easter Sunday, in the church, conf on
Apr 16 1911, Easter Sunday, by Alfred Rodman Hussey pp 92, 66

MUDGE Priscilla Phillips m to Evan N. Rinehart on Sep 8 1917, both of
Baltimore, Charles A. Wing officiating p 137

MUDGE Sally Ann dau of A. B. and C. C. Mudge, b Dec 20 1847, bapt Feb 13 1848
p 33

MUDGE Sally Ann m to William Foy Knox on Feb 12 1873 at the church at 12:00
noon, both of Baltimore, m during the ministry of C. K. Weld and by him p 125

MUNCKS Marie E. m to William R. Cole on Nov 7 1854 p 115

MUNROE Mary E. m to John J. Brown on Sep 15 1845 p 110

MUNROE Sarah Lee m to George Endicot on Dec 18 1828, both of Baltimore p 105
MURPHY Mary Jane m to William Hill on Jan 19 1854 p 114
MURRAY Aquila B. m to Florence M. Fowler on Feb 8 1821 of Baltimore p 102
MURRAY Aquila B. and Florence M. p of Mary Jane p 13, Susan Elizabeth p 13
MURRAY Mary Jane dau of Aquila B. and Florence M. Murray, bapt on Dec 31
    1824 p 13
MURRAY Susan Elizabeth dau of Aquila B. and Florence M. Murray, bapt on
    Dec 31 1824 p 13
MYERS Anna C. m to Joshua W. Coolidge of Baltimore on Feb 11 1912 at 2:15 p.m.,
    at 1314 Bolton Street; Miss Myers was from Pen Mar PA p 135
MYERS James Edwin m to Annette Corner on Mar 31 1883 at the residence of
    Solomon Corner, on the corner of Biddle and Calvert Streets p 126
MYERS James Edwin b Oct 15 1840, d May 31 1919, funeral Jun 2 1919, Charles A.
    Wing officiating p 96
MYERS James Edwin and Annette Corner p of Mary Calvert Myers p 60
MYERS Mary Calvert dau of J. Edwin and Annette C. Myers, b Dec 7 1883, bapt
    May 11 1884, Sunday, in church p 60
NASH Mary Blunt dau of Solon and Mary Blunt Nash, b Apr 30 1833, bapt May 28
    1842 p 28
NASH Sarah Elizabeth dau of Solon and Mary Blunt Nash, b Mar 15 1835, bapt
    May 28 1843 p 28
NASH Solon and Mary Blunt Nash p of Mary Blunt p 28, Sarah Elizabeth p 28
NAYLOR Henry L. m to Mary S. Mudge on Dec 5 1894 at 12 noon in the church p 131
NAYLOR Henry Louis and Mary S. (Mudge) Naylor p of Louis Hastings p 71
NAYLOR Louis Hastings son of Henry Louis and Mary S. (Mudge) Naylor, b Jul 4
    1896, bapt Jun 6 1897, Whitsunday, in the church p 71
NEIHEISER, Andrew G. and Christiana D. (Bernhard) p of Credilla Weld p 64,
    Irvin Leonard p 69
NEIHEISER Credilla Weld dau of Andrew G. and Christiana D. (Bernhard) Neiheiser
    b Jun 27 1890 in Germantown PA, bapt Oct 26 1890 in the church p 64
NEIHEISER Irvin Leonard son of Andrew G. and Christiana D. (Bernhard) Neiheiser
    b Dec 23 1893 in Germantown PA, bapt May 13 1894 during Whitsunday service
    p 69
NEWTON Sargent listed as a comm of the church in Sep 1869 p 82
NICHOLS Frank Loring m to May Cole on Feb 17 1904 at her home in Mount
    Washington, Baltimore County, at 6:15 p.m. (the bride's parents were the
    late William R. and Maria E. Cole); Mr. Nichols was from Washington DC,
    Alfred Rodman Hussey officiating p 133
NITZE Carl Louis conf and joined the church on Jun 6 1897, Whitsunday p 88
NITZE Carl Louis and Mathilde V. p of Vietor, b Jun 26 1925 p 77
NITZE Vietor son of Carl Louis and Mathilde V. Nitze, b Jun 26 1925, bapt
    Sep 27 1925 during the ministry of Rev. Charles G. Girelius p 77
NOLAN Jacob J.M. m to Katie A. Burns on Jun 29 1892 in the chapel, both of
    Shmokin PA p 130
OBERG Gulli J. m to James C. Callowhill of Boston on Jun 1 1894 at 9:00 a.m.
    in the church; Miss Oberg was from Stockholm, Sweden p 131
OGIER Eliza m to John W. Robinson on May 10 1832, both of Baltimore p 106
OGLESBY John G. of Atlanta GA, m to Nina, dau of the late Frederick Caspari
    of Baltimore on Nov 9 1907 at 7:00 p.m. in Govans, Baltimore County p 134
OLIVER George m to Mary Cunningham on Sep 6 1846 p 111
OREM Colonel J. M. at his home in Baltimore County on Apr 26 1877, Sophie G.
    Rose m Charles V. Merridith of Richmond VA at 12:30 p.m.; Miss Rose was
    from Baltimore County p 125

ORRIS Claudia K. m to Harry A. McCorkle of Baltimore on Apr 16 1910 at 6:30
    p.m., at 1314 Bolton Street; Miss Oris was from Johnstown PA, Alfred R.
    Hussey officiating p 135
OSBORNE Georgey Miss bapt as an adult on Nov 15 1854, listed as a comm of
    the church in 1865 p 41, 78
OSBORNE John m to Lucretia Bartlett both of Baltimore, on Mar 30 1828 by
    J.H.L. Blanchard p 103
OSBORNE Martha Godfrey bapt as an adult on Nov 15 1854, m to John T. Uthman
    on Nov 16 1854 pp 41, 115
OSGOOD Charles Christopher son of Henry and ------Osgood, bapt Mar 22 1821 p 6
OSGOOD Franklin son of R(obert) H. and Sarah Osgood, bapt Dec 14 1828 p 14
OSGOOD George Archer son of Robert H. and Sarah Osgood, bapt May 15 1821 p 6
OSGOOD Henry and Wife p of Mary Elizabeth p 3, Henry Bryant p 3, Charles
    Christopher p 6
OSGOOD Henry Bryant son of Henry and ------Osgood, bapt Jun 22 1819 p 3
OSGOOD Mary Elizabeth dau of Henry and ------Osgood, bapt Jun 22 1819 p 3
OSGOOD Robert H. and Sarah p of Robert Hawkins p 4, George Archer p 6,
    William Henry p 10, Franklin p 14
OSGOOD Robert Hawkins son of Robert H. and Sarah Osgood, bapt Sep 19 1819 p 4
OSGOOD William Henry son of Robert H. and Sarah Osgood, bapt Jan 12 1823 p 10
PALMER Elsie m to Thomas J. Brown on Oct 17 1894 at 6 p.m. in the church;
    Mr. Brown was from Washington, Miss Palmer from Baltimore p 131
PALMER Janet McP. m to Robert E. Robinson on Nov 17 1897 at 6:30 p.m.,
    Wednesday, in the church; Mr. Robinson was from Philadelphia, Miss Palmer
    was from Baltimore p 132
PALMQUIST Maria bapt on May 21 1893 in the chapel, b Mar 25 1870 in Stockholm
    Sweden p 67
PARKER Euphemia Moris dau of William and Lucy C. Parker, b Oct 10 1852, bapt
    Mar 27 1853 p 39
PARKER George Byron son of William and Emiline Cole Parker, b Jan 27 1833,
    bapt Jun 2 1833 p 18
PARKER William and Emiline Cole p of William Roswell p 17, George Byron p 18
PARKER William and Lucy C. p of Euphemia p 39
PARKER William Roswell son of William and Emiline Cole Parker, b May 23 1831,
    bapt Mar 4 1832 p 17
PARLETT Charles J. m to Henrietta M. Pensch, both of Baltimore, on Jun 15 1904
    at 9 a.m. in the church, Alfred Rodman Hussey officiating p 133
PARRISH Mittie Emma dau of William and Elizabeth Parrish, b Nov 10 1874, bapt
    Dec 10 1874 p 53
PARRISH William and Elizabeth p of Mittie Emma p 53
PATON Robert Townley son of Stewart and Frances Margaret Halsey Paton, b Apr
    7 1901, bapt Jun 9 1903 at 213 West Monument Street during the ministry of
    Alfred Rodman Hussey p 72
PATON Stewart and Frances Margaret Halsey p of Richard Townley p 72
PATTERSON Anna St. Clair Gerry dau of the late Arthur Melville and Alice
    Gerry Patterson, b Nov 4 1875, bapt May 2 1880 in the church p 57
PATTERSON Arthur Melville and Alice Gerry p of Anna St. Clair Gerry p 57
PATTERSON Lavinia (see also Patterson, Leonora) m to Robert Bines on Jun 2
    1836, both of Baltimore p 107
PEALE Angelica m to John D. Godman on Oct 6 1821, both of Baltimore p 102
PEARCE Catherine Russell dau of Charles R. and Emiline Pearce, b Dec 28 1835
    bapt Nov 23 1848 p 34
PEARCE Charles A. and Emiline p of Henry Sumner p 16, Rebecca Russell p 16

PEARCE Charles R. and Emiline p of Emily p 19, Catherine Russell p 34, Elizabeth Vassell p 34, Emma Degen p 34

PEARCE Charles Russell m to Emeline Sumner on Nov 11 1825 p 103

PEARCE Elizabeth Vassell dau of Charles R. and Emiline Pearce, b Apr 9 1838, bapt Nov 23 1848, listed as a comm of the church in Sep 1869 pp 34, 81

PEARCE Emily dau of Charles R. and Emiline Pearce, bapt May 24 1835 p 19

PEARCE Emma Degen dau of Charles R. and Emiline Pearce, b Dec 5 1840, bapt Nov 23 1848 p 34

PEARCE Henry Sumner son of Charles A. and Emiline Pearce, bapt May 22 1831 p 16

PEARCE Rebecca Russell dau of Charles A. and Emiline Pearce, bapt May 22 1831 p 16

PENDLETON Marguerite conf on Easter Sunday Apr 27 1912 by Alfred Rodman Hussey p 93

PENDLETON Wirt Wentworth conf on Easter Sunday Apr 27 1912 by Alfred Rodman Hussey p 93

PENNIMAN Susan Ann m to Moses Swett of New York on Sep 24 1833; Miss Penniman was from Baltimore p 107

PENNIMAN William m to Henrietta Griffith on Jul 10 1819, both of Baltimore p 101

PENSCH Henrietta Marie Caroline conf on Good Friday Apr 12 1895, joined the church on Easter Sunday Apr 14 1895, m Charles J. Parlett on Jun 15 1904 at 9 a.m. in the church, Alfred Rodman Hussey officiating pp 87, 133

PERKINS Richard K. m to Amanda M. Pierce on Nov 8 1866 p 122

PERRY George Leonard son of Leonard and ------Perry, b Apr 19 1842, bapt Jul 16 1854 p 41

PERRY Henrietta Tyson m to Malcolm Goodridge on Jun 30 1898 by Rev. William R. Lord p 132

PERRY Ira John m to Helen Walsh of Philadelphia PA on Nov 19 1914 at 1:15 p.m. at 221 West Center Street; Mr. Perry was from St. Louis MO, Alfred Rodman Hussey officiating p 136

PERRY Leonard and Wife p of George Leonard p 41

PETRI Nina R. m to Orin C. Trow on Jun 8 1858 p 117

PFIFFERKORN Edna m to Robert H. McCawley of Hagerstown PA on Sep 18 1912 at 2 p.m. in the church; Miss Pfifferkorn was from Baltimore, Alfred Rodman Hussey officiating p 136

PFITSCH Alfred m to Emma B. Kaaz on Thanksgiving Day Nov 28 1889 at 8 p.m. in the church, p of Edgar Kaaz p 66, Irene Ada p 70, p 128

PFITSCH Edgar Kaaz son of Alfred and Emma B. Kaaz Pfitsch, b Aug 21 1892, bapt Nov 6 1892 p 66

PFITSCH Irene Ada dau of Alfred and Emma B. Kaaz Pfitsch, b Aug 15 1894, bapt Dec 23 1894 p 70

PFITSH Alfred (see also Pfitsch, Alfred) son of Alfred and Emma Bertha Henrietta Kaaz Pfitsh (Pfitsch), b Sep 14 1890, bapt Oct 15 1890 p 64

PHILLIPS A.B. Mrs. listed as a comm of the church in 1865 p 78

PHILLIPS Catherine Caroline dau of Isaac and Anne Phillips, bapt Feb 15 1821, m to Abner B. Mudge on Apr 26 1843 pp 5, 110

PHILLIPS Isaac and Anne p of Isaac p 5, Catherine Caroline p 5, Sally Ann p 11, Priscilla p 14

PHILLIPS Louis J. conf on Easter Sunday Apr 13 1884 during the ministry of Charles Richmond Weld, m to Margaret E. L. Reichart on Jan 3 1890 at 12:00 noon in the church, both of Baltimore pp 85, 129

PHILLIPS Mary Grace dau of Thomas and Ann Phillips, b Jun 1 1851, bapt Sep 25 1853 p 40

PHILLIPS Priscilla dau of Isaac and Anne Phillips, bapt Oct 1 1828, listed as a comm of the church in 1865 pp 14, 78

PHILLIPS Sally Ann dau of Isaac and Anne Phillips, bapt on Dec 12 1823 by F. W.P. Greenwood p 11

PHILLIPS Theresa J. conf during the ministry of Charles Richmond Weld on Easter Sunday Apr 13 1884, m to Edwin R. Freeburger on Jul 8 1885 at 6:00 p.m. in the church, both of Baltimore pp 85, 127

PHILLIPS Thomas and Ann p of Mary Grace p 40

PHIPPS Samuel m to Mary Anne Kennedy of Baltimore on Sep 27 1841; Mr. Phipps was from Roxbury MA p 109

PIERCE Amanda M. m to Richard K. Perkins on Nov 8 1866 by John F.W. Ware p 122

PINKNEY Emily m to Richard A. Jones on Mar 28 1831, both of Baltimore p 104

PITT Charles F. Jr. m to Kate B. Rose of the county at the home of Col. J.M. Orem in Baltimore County, on Thursday Apr 26 1877 at 12:30 p.m.; Mr. Pitt was from the city p 126

PITT Charles Faris and Kate Barker (Rose) p of Sophie Rose p 55, Kate Barker p 59, Charles Gordon p 70-1/2

PITT Charles Gordon son of Charles Faris Pitt and Kate Barker (Rose) Pitt, b Sep 12 1896 at Catonsville MD, bapt Apr 18 1897 Easter Sunday in the church p 70-1/2

PITT Kate Barker b Mar 19 1883, d Apr 10 1921, buried Apr 12 1921, Harry Foster Burns officiating p 98

PITT Kate Barker dau of Charles Faris Pitt Jr. and Kate Barker (Rose) Pitt, b Mar 19 1883, bapt Jun 20 1883 at Ridge Lawn in Baltimore County MD p 59

PITT Sophie Rose dau of Charles Faris Pitt Jr. and Kate Barker (Rose) Pitt, b Jan 27 1878, bapt Jun 9 1878, Whitsunday, at 412 Eutaw Place p 55

PLATER William of Saint Mary's County (Charles County?), m Maria Louisa Hobby of Baltimore on Jul 22 1837 p 108

POOR Abby dau of John Henry and Jane Poor, bapt on Apr 2 1821, m to William E. Mayhew on Dec 3 1856 pp 6, 116

POOR Cornelia m to Brantz Mayer on Nov 15 1848 p 112

POOR Frances J. m to William E. Mayhew on Jun 10 1844 p 110

POOR J. E. Mrs. listed as a comm of the church in 1865 p 78

POOR Jane Mrs. listed as a comm of the church in Sep 1869 p 81

POOR John Henry son of John Henry and Jane Poor, bapt on Nov 18 1821 p 7

POOR John Henry bapt on Apr 2 1821 p 6

POOR John Henry and Jane p of Abby p 6, dau (name unknown) p 6, John Henry p 7, Virginia p 26

POOR Kate listed as a comm of the church in 1865 and in 1869 pp 78, 81

POOR Virginia dau of John Henry and Jane Poor, b Aug 10 1827, bapt Dec 5 1841, listed as a comm of the church in 1865 pp 26, 78

POPE Daniel F. m to Hannah M. Schaeff on Apr 23 1857 p 116

POPPLEIN Grace Campbell dau of John Thompson Popplein and Matilda Girvier (Campbell) Popplein, b Jan 17 1873, bapt Jan 14 1874 at 108 McCullough during the ministry of Charles Richmond Weld p 52

POPPLEIN John Thompson and Matilda Girvier (Campbell) Popplein p of Grace Campbell p 52, William Campbell p 54

POPPLEIN William Campbell son of John Thompson Popplein and Matilda Girvier (Campbell) Popplein, b Jun 14 1875, bapt Mar 6 1876 at 108 McCullough Street p 54

POTTS Hamilton m to Louisa R. Sterrett on Jun 1 1844 p 110

POWER William m to Elizabeth A. Frick on Oct 14 1847 p 112

PRATT Enoch listed as a comm of the church in 1865 and in 1869, m to Maria Louisa Hyde on Aug 1 1837, both of Baltimore pp 78, 81, 108

PRATT Maria L. Mrs. listed as a comm of the church in Sep 1869 p 81
PRENTISS Clifton Kennedy son of John and Amelia Prentiss, b Jun 16 1835,
    bapt Jul 18 1835 p 20
PRENTISS John and Amelia p of Thomas M. p 20, William Scolley p 20, Clifton
    Kennedy p 20, William p 27, Mary Amelia p 27
PRENTISS Mary Amelia dau of John and Amelia Prentiss, b Aug 11 1842, bapt
    Dec 17 1842 p 27
PRENTISS Thomas M. (?) son of John and Amelia Prentiss, b Oct 26 1829, bapt
    Jul 18 1835 p 20
PRENTISS William son of John and Amelia Prentiss, b May 29 1839, bapt Dec 17
    1842 p 27
PRENTISS William Scolley son of John and Amelia Prentiss, b Jul 10 1833, bapt
    Jul 18 1835 p 20
PUGH Ethel m to Robert J. Bell on Feb 26 1902 at 10:00 a.m. at 1 West Hamilton
    Street, both of Norfolk VA, Alfred R. Hussey officiating p 134
PUGH Laura m to Samuel Shepherd on Dec 19 1839, both of Baltimore p 108
PUNDERSON Nicholas Robert son of Nicholas Williamson Kneass and Laura Virginia
    Punderson, b Jan 26 1894, bapt Nov 24 1896 at 607 North Charles Street p 71
PUNDERSON Nicholas Williamson Kneass and Laura Virginia Punderson, p of
    Nicholas Robert p 71
PURDY William A. m to Mary McNulty on Oct 17 1850 p 113
QUINBY (Quimby?) Jacob Hook bapt Jan 18 1838, aged 31 p 23
RANSTEAD Charles and Harriett Willard p of Kate Alice p 54
RANSTEAD Kate Alice dau of Charles and Harriett Willard Ranstead, b in
    Boston MA on Feb 15 1857, bapt and conf on Whitsunday May 20 1877, in the
    church during the ministry of Charles Richmond Weld pp 54, 85
RANSTEAD Mrs. listed as a comm of the church on Jan 1 1870 p 82
RAUB Ann Maria m to Alexander Young on Feb 24 1847 p 111
RAUCH Charles R. m to Georgia Emmart on Feb 26 1889 at 1326 Argyle Avenue,
    both of Baltimore p 128
RAUCH Charles R. and Georgia (Emmart) p of Charles William p 64, Helena
    Catherine p 69, Stewart Emmart p 69
RAUCH Charles William son of Charles R. and Georgia (Emmart), b Dec 18 1889,
    bapt May 14 1890 p 64
RAUCH Helena Catharine dau of Charles R(udolf) and Georgia (Emmart) Rauch,
    b Jul 5 1891, bapt Nov 19 1894 in the church p 69
RAUCH Stewart Emmart son of Charles Rudolf and Georgia (Emmart) Rauch, b
    Jun 30 1894, bapt Nov 19 1894 p 69
READY Harriet Isabella dau of John and Elizabeth Ready, b Jan 31 1818, bapt
    Nov 3 1822 p 9
READY John and Elizabeth p of Sarah Amanda p 9, Harriet Isabella p 9,
    Octavia p 9
READY Octavia dau of John and Elizabeth Ready, b Mar 11 1821, bapt Nov 3
    1822 p 9
READY Sarah Amanda dau of John and Elizabeth Ready, b Nov 28 1815, bapt
    Nov 3 1822 p 9
REED Margaret A. of New York, m to Warren H. Lewis of Baltimore on May 23
    1910 at 3 p.m. at Cedar Lawn, Govans MD, Alfred R. Hussey officiating p 135
REED Samuel Payson son of Seth and ------Reed, bapt May 24 1835 p 9
REED Seth and ------ p of Samuel Payson p 9
REICHART Margaret E.L. m to Louis J. Philipp on Jan 3 1890 at 12 M. in the
    church, both of Baltimore p 129
REMINGTON William m to Caroline H.B. Williams on Feb 10 1846 p 111

RENALT(?) Carroll Melchere dau of J.J. and Susie Renalt, b in Baltimore May 5 1904, bapt Feb 12 1911 in the church p 73

RENALT(?) J.J. and Susie M. p of Valerette p 73, Carroll Melchere p 73

RENALT Valerette Muessebrock (see also Renalt, Laberette Musselbrock) dau of J.J. and Susie Renalt, b in Charleston SC Dec 1 1892, bapt Feb 12 1911 in the church p 73

RENICK Richard M. (see also Renwick, Richard M.) m to Anne R. Conner on Jun 15 1841 p 109

RENWICK Isabel Hamilton dau of Richard M. and Anne R. Renwick, b Apr 17 1842, bapt May 14 1845 p 30

RENWICK Richard M. and Anne R. p of Isabel Hamilton p 30, Robert Pyke p 30, William Herbert p 30

RENWICK Robert Pyke son of Richard M. and Anne R. Renwick, b May 26 1843, bapt May 14 1845 p 30

RENWICK William Herbert son of Richard M. and Anne R. Renwick, b in Feb 1845, bapt May 14 1845 p 30

RETEN William m to Miss Rebecca Mahaney on May 13 1819, both of Baltimore p 101

REUMAN Mary F. m to Joseph F. Scheerer on Jul 14 1891 in the church p 129

REVERE Frederick Balestier son of John and Lydia Le Baron Revere, bapt May 16 1824, Mr. F.W.P. Greenwood officiating p 12

REVERE John and Lydia Le Baron p of Frederick Balestier p 12

RHOADS Charles son of Willard Rhoads and Wife, b Jan 11 1820, bapt Nov 11 1831 p 16

RHOADS John son of Willard Rhoads and Wife, b Jul 11 1818, bapt Nov 11 1831 p 16

RHOADS Rebecca dau of Willard Rhoads and Wife, b Oct 2 1816, bapt Nov 11 1831 p 16

RHOADS Willard and Wife (Lucy) p of Rebecca p 16, John p 16, Charles p 16

RHODES Benjamin C. and Wife (Mary Luscomb) (see also Rhoads) p of Benjamin Merrill p 18, William Luscomb p 18, Mary Elizabeth p 18, Sarah p 18, Charles Henry p 18, John Marshall p 21, Martha Luscomb p 26

RHODES Benjamin Merrill son of Benjamin C. Rhodes and Wife, b Jun 6 1823, bapt Nov 27 1833 p 18

RHODES Charles Henry son of Benjamin C. Rhodes and Wife, b Oct 15 1833, bapt Nov 27 1833 p 18

RHODES John Marshall son of Benjamin C. Rhodes and Wife, b Apr 1 1835, bapt Dec 13 1835 p 21

RHODES Martha Luscomb dau of Benjamin C. Rhodes and Wife, b Jan 7 1838, bapt May 19 1842 p 26

RHODES Mary Elizabeth dau of Benjamin C. Rhodes and Wife, b Aug 1826, bapt Nov 27 1833 p 18

RHODES Sarah dau of Benjamin C. Rhodes and Wife, bapt May 2 1833 p 18

RHODES William Luscomb son of Benjamin C. Rhodes and Wife, b Jan 26 1825, bapt Nov 27 1833 p 18

RICHARDSON Harry D. conf on Whitsunday May 15 1910, Alfred Rodman Hussey officiating p 92

RICHMOND Mary E. conf and joined the church on Palm Sunday, Apr 14 1889 p 86

RIDER Alexander and Mary p of Helen Tiffany p 57, Mary Helen p 59

RIDER Helen Tiffany dau of Mary and Alexander Rider, b May 6 1879, bapt on Jun 1 1879 Whitsunday in the church p 57

RIDER Mary Helen dau of Mary and Alexander Rider, bapt Jun 12 1881 in the church p 59

RIEBLING Charles Alvin son of Charles A. Riebling and Marian Katharine (Croh) Riebling, b Mar 23 1911, bapt Nov 19 1911 in the church p 73

RIEBLING Charles Alvin conf on Whitsunday Jun 11 1905 by Alfred Rodman Hussey p 91

RIEBLING Charles Alvin and Marian Katharine (Croh) Riebling, p of Charles Alvin p 73, Marian Elizabeth p 74

RIEBLING Charles Oliver (see also Riebling, Charles Alvin) pp 73, 91

RIEBLING Fred conf on Easter Sunday 1900 p 88

RIEBLING Lillian Theresa conf on Good Friday, Apr 12 1895, joined the church on Easter Sunday Apr 14 1895 p 87

RIEBLING Marian Elizabeth dau of Marian Katharine Riebling and Charles Alvin Riebling, b Jul 20 1915, bapt Dec 12 1915 in the church p 74

RIMPH Electra J. m Caesar A. Brown on Jun 13 1850 p 113

RINEHART Evan N. m on Sep 8 1917 to Priscilla P. Mudge, both of Baltimore, Charles A. Wing officiating, p of Margaret Phillips p 75

RINEHART Margaret Phillips dau of Priscilla Phillips (Mudge) Rinehart and Evan N.(?) Rinehart, b May 28 1918, bapt Dec 29 1918 p 75

RINGLEB Henry and Mary p of William Henry p 40

RINGLEB William Henry son of Henry and Mary Ringleb, b Jan 21 1853, bapt Nov 23 1853 p 40

RIVERA Mary F. m to Quney A. Hooper on Dec 28 1856 p 116

RIXSE Anne Margaret (see also River, Anne Margaret) conf on Good Friday, Apr 12 1895, joined the church on Easter Sunday Apr 14 1895 p 87

RIXSE Louise (see also River, Louise) conf and joined the church on May 21 1893, b Sep 16 1875 p 87

RIXSE Mary Louise m to Charles Louis Welke on Sep 25 1898, Rev. William R. Cole of Cohasset MA officiating p 132

RIXSE Sarah Jane conf and joined the church on Jun 6 1897, Whitsunday p 88

ROBERT Sanderson m to Mary B. Bevan on Mar 28 1848 p 112

ROBERTS Mrs. listed as a comm of the church in 1865 p 78

ROBINSON Abby S. Mrs. listed as a comm of the church in Sep 1869 p 81

ROBINSON Ann Maria b Jun 6 1836, bapt Dec 20 1839, dau of William C. and Abby S. Robinson p 24

ROBINSON Edward Ayrault son of William C. and Abby S. Robinson, b Sep 27 1838, bapt Dec 20 1839, m on Nov 14 1871 to Alice Canby at the home of Thomas G. Canby on Dolphin Street, at 4:00 p.m., during the ministry of E.C. Guild pp 24, 123

ROBINSON John W. m to Eliza Ogien on May 10 1832, both of Baltimore p 106

ROBINSON Mrs. listed as a comm of the church in 1865 p 79

ROBINSON Robert E. m to Janet McP. Palmer of Baltimore on Nov 17 1897 at 6:30 p.m., Wednesday, in the church, Mr. Robinson was from Philadelphia p 132

ROBINSON William m to Anne Steele on May 4 1831, both of Baltimore p 106

ROBINSON William Ayrault son of William C. and Abby S. Robinson, b Apr 18 1834, bapt Jul 27 1834 at Newport RI p 19

ROBINSON William C. and Abby S. p of William Ayrault p 19, Ann Maria p 24, Edward Ayrault p 24, William Shaw p 26

ROBINSON William Shaw son of William C. and Abby Robinson, b Dec 3 1840, bapt Jun 13 1841 p 26

ROGGE Angelica m to Carl George Hilgenberg on Jan 11 1898 at 6:00 p.m., Tuesday, in the church, both of Baltimore, Albert Walkley officiating p 132

ROHR Hulda R. m to Thomley W. Martin of New York on Oct 5 1904 at 12 Noon, at 1500 Linden Avenue, Alfred R. Hussey officiating; Miss Rohr was from Baltimore p 134

ROLANDO Anne Hepburn dau of Henry and Anne Elizabeth Rolando, b Aug 12 1853, bapt Nov 27 1853 p 40

ROLANDO Henry and Ann Elizabeth (Buckler) m Apr 29 1851, p of Mary Provaine(?) p 38, Anne Hepburn p 40, John Buckler p 45

ROLANDO John Buckler son of Henry and Anne Elizabeth Rolando, b Jan 12 1857, bapt Apr 28 1857 p 45

ROLANDO Mary Provaine(?) dau of Henry and Ann Elizabeth Rolando, b May 30 1852, bapt Jul 10 1852 p 38

ROMOSER Alexander Frederick and Mary Elizabeth p of Eva Spangler p 60, Emma Virginia Lee p 60, Thomas Andrew Hendricks p 62

ROMOSER Emma Virginia Lee dau of Alexander Frederick and Mary Elizabeth Romoser, b Aug 23 1883, bapt Jun 1 1884, Whitsunday, in the church p 60

ROMOSER Eva Spangler dau of Alexander Frederick and Mary Elizabeth Romoser, b Dec 9 1880, bapt Jun 1 1884 p 60

ROMOSER Thomas Andrew Hendricks son of Alexander Frederick and Mary Elizabeth Romoser, b Apr 7 1886, bapt Jun 5 1887 in the church p 62

ROSE John m Margaret Mac Cormac, of Belfast, Ireland, on May 19 1909 at 1:15 p.m. at 1314 Bolton Street, Alfred R. Hussey officiating; Mr. Rose was from Philadelphia p 135

ROSE John and Sophie p of Sophia Gooding p 40, Kate Barker p 40

ROSE Kate Barker dau of John and Sophie G. Rose, b Apr 24 1853, bapt Jun 1853 p 40

ROSE Ruth B. m to Charles F. Pitt Jr. of Baltimore on Apr 26 1877 at 12:30 p.m. at the home of Col. J.M. Orem in Baltimore County; Miss Rose was from Baltimore County p 126

ROSE Sophie Gooding dau of John and Sophie G. Rose, b Dec 12 1851, bapt Jun 1853 p 40

ROUSE Katharine Elizabeth (erratum: see Lampher, Katharine Elizabeth) dau of Elizabeth P. (Sauer) and Raymond Lampher, b in 1908, bapt Jun 7 1908, Whitsunday, in the church p 73

ROUSE Raymond W. Lampher and Regina P. (Sauer) (erratum: see Lampher, Raymond W. and Regina P. (Sauer) p of Katharine Elizabeth p 73, Charlotte Alice p 74

ROWE Harry Man m to Jaennette Steigelmann on Jan 6 1915 at 10:00 a.m., at Woodlawn in Baltimore County, Alfred R. Hussey officiating p 36

RUCKLE John N. listed as a comm of the church in Sep 1869 p 82

RUDOLPH Elizabeth m to Howard H. League on Nov 17 1893 at 8:00 p.m., in the chapel p 130

RUFFERSBERGER Bertha conf on Whitsunday May 30 1909 by Alfred Rodman Hussey p 92

RUSSELL Arabella m to Cleveland P. Manning on Jun 5 1888 in the church at 12:00 noon, both of Baltimore p 128

RUSSELL Francis Albert son of William and Susan Gates Russell, b Aug 10 1850, bapt Jan 31 1851 p 36

RUSSELL Martha dau of Robert C. and Martha Russell, b Jul 25 1850, bapt Jan 29 1851 p 36

RUSSELL Robert C. and Martha p of Martha p 36

RUSSELL Susan Gates Maynard m to William Russell on Dec 24 1845 p 111

RUSSELL William (?) son of William and Susan Gates Russell, b Apr 15 1848, bapt Jan 31 1851 p 36

RUSSELL William and Susan Gates Maynard p of Francis Albert p 36, William (?) p 36

RYNEX Eliza Caswell m to Thomas Rinaldo Johnson on Feb 12 1846 p 111

SALZER Lillie m to Franz Euler on Nov 16 1887 at 6:00 p.m. in the church p 127

SAMS Charlotte Eliza (see also Samz, Charlotte E.) b Feb 22 1821, bapt Apr 2 1821 p 6

SAMUELS Edwin F. and Kate ------Samuels p of Lloyd Samuels p 73

SAMUELS Lloyd son of Edwin F. and Kate ------Samuels, b Aug 12 1908, bapt Apr 11 1909, Easter Sunday, in the church p 73

SAUER Dorothy Daubert dau of ------(Daubert) Sauer and Werner Sauer, b in 1912, bapt Jun 11 1912 at 1900(?) Harlem Avenue p 74

SAUER Justus b May 18 1829, d Feb 5 1918, funeral Feb 8 1918, Charles A. Wing officiating p 96

SAUER Katie conf on Whitsunday May 31 1903, Alfred Rodman Hussey officiating p 90

SAUER Lena conf on Easter Sunday 1900 p 88

SAUER Regina P. m to Raymond W. Lampher on Apr 30 1907 at 4:00 p.m. at 1314 Bolton Street, both of Baltimore, Alfred R. Hussey officiating p 134

SAUER Werner and ------(Daubert) Sauer p of Dorothy Daubert p 74

SCHAEFF Hannah M. m to Daniel F. Pope on Apr 23 1857 p 116

SCHEERER Joseph F. m Mary F. Neuman on Jul 14 1891 in the church p 129

SCHETTER Frederick son of Frederick and Charlotte Schetter, b Oct 13 1831, bapt Apr 14 1833 p 17

SCHETTER Frederick and Charlotte p of Frederick p 17, Otto p 17

SCHETTER Otto son of Frederick and Charlotte Schetter, b Dec 27 1832, bapt Apr 14 1833 p 17

SCHEUTER Frederick L. (Schluter?) conf and joined the church on Apr 14 1889, Palm Sunday p 86

SCHLENS, Veronica of Baltimore, m Charles auf dem Brink of Germantown on Apr 25 1894 at 7:30 p.m. in the church p 131

SCHLUTER Frederick A.L. m Alice Abraham on Mar 21 1894 at 12 noon in the church, both of Baltimore p 131

SCHMIDT Mary Schubert conf on Whitsunday May 19 1907, Alfred Rodman Hussey officiating p 91

SCHWEINSBERG Dorothea dau of George and Lena Schweinsberg, b May 16 1895, bapt Nov 10 1895 p 70

SCHWEINSBERG George and Lena p of Dorothea p 70

SCHWEINSBERG George W. and Caroline Neubert p of Ida Lovell p 67

SCHWEINSBERG Gladys Edythe dau of Lula Anna and John G. Schweinsberg, b Jan 5 1914, bapt Feb 22 1914 in the church p 74

SCHWEINSBERG Ida Lovell dau of George W. and Caroline (Neubert) Schweinsberg, b Feb 18 1893 in Baltimore, bapt during Whitsunday service May 23 1893 p 67

SCHWEINSBERG Ida Lovell dau of Lula Anna and John George Schweinsberg, b Mar 16 1912, bapt Apr 28 1912 in the church p 74

SCHWEINSBERG Lula Anna and John G. p of Ida Lovell p 74, Gladys Edythe p 74

SEDGWICK Harry T. m Jessie Basil on Apr 28 1919, both of Baltimore, Charles A. Wing officiating p 137

SEMPERS Rev. Charles T. bapt the Ellsworth children, Florence and Elmer, dau and son of Martin and Louisa League Ellsworth on Apr 28 1893 in the chapel p 66

SEYMOUR Arabella conf during the ministry of Charles Richmond Weld on Jun 8 1878 p 85

SEYMOUR Bertha Lee conf during the ministry of Charles Richmond Weld on May 20 1877 and also bapt on this day, b in Baltimore in 1862 p 54

SHAW Ann C. m to Osmond C. Tiffany on Jul 17 1822, both of Baltimore p 103

SHAW Ann Maria m to William B. Butler on May 5 1858 p 116

SHAW Rebecca Jane dau of William C. and Ann Maria Shaw, bapt Jun 1 1822 p 8
SHAW William C. and Anna Maria p of Rebecca Jane p 8, William Chickley
(Checkley?) p 8
SHAW William Chickley (Checkley?) son of William C. and Ann Maria Shaw, bapt
Jul 4 1824 p 12
SHELTON Margaret Elizabeth dau of William H. and Margaret Green Shelton, b
Jan 14 1899, bapt Apr 2 1899, Easter Sunday, in the church, Theodore C.
Williams officiating p 71
SHELTON William H. and Margaret Green Shelton p of Margaret Elizabeth p 71
SHEPHERD Samuel m to Lara Pugh on Dec 19 1839, both of Baltimore p 108
SHERWOOD William C. m to Rosetta G. Friebus(?) on Jan 22 1912 at 103
Beechdale Drive, Roland Park, at 12:00 noon, Alfred Rodman Hussey
officiating, Mr. Sherwood was from New York, Miss Friebus(?) of Washington
DC p 135
SHIPLEY Jared Sparks son of William and Sarah Ann Shipley, b Nov 11 1822,
bapt Dec 2 1822 p 9
SHIPLEY Johnzee Sellman child of William and Sarah Ann Shipley, b Mar 13 1819,
bapt Dec 2 1822 p 9
SHIPLEY Joseph Priestly Hall son of William and Sarah Ann Shipley, b Oct 27
1820, bapt Dec 2 1822 p 9
SHIPLEY William and Sarah Ann p of Johnzee Sellman p 9, Joseph Priestly Hall
p 9, Jared Sparks p 9
SHIPPEN Rev'd Rush R. officiated at the wedding of Thomas Kell Bradford and
Jane Mayer on Jun 14 1883 at 16 McCullogh Street in the absence of C.K.
Weld, Rev'd Shippen was from Washington p 127
SIMON Adolphe and Margaret p of Roberta Lee p 130
SIMON Charles and Helene p of Minna R. p 129
SIMON Emma E. m to George H. Vocke on Nov 4 1886 at 1:30 p.m. in the church,
both of Baltimore p 127
SIMON Evelina C. conf on Whitsunday Jun 11 1905 by Alfred Rodman Hussey p 91
SIMON Margaret Louise m to Frank Mudge on Jun 13 1888 at 8:00 p.m. in the
church p 128
SIMON Minna dau of Charles and Helene Simon of Baltimore, m to Hentey T.
Fernald at 1119 Linden Avenue on Jul 9 1890 at 8:00 p.m.; Mr. Fernald was
from Massachusetts p 129
SIMON Roberta Lee dau of Adolphe and Margaret (Torney) Simon, conf and joined
the church on Palm Sunday, Apr 14 1889, m to Joseph C. France on Sep 24
1892 at 11:15 a.m. in the church's chapel, both of Baltimore pp 86, 130
SLADE Annie Wheeler (see also Slad) dau of Edward and Ellen W. Slade, b
Jan 7 1851, bapt Apr 10 1851 p 37
SLADE Edward son of Edward and Ellen W. Slade, b Jul 15 1856, bapt Oct 16 1856
p 44
SLADE Edward and Ellen W. p of Annie Wheeler p 37, Frances p 40, Edward p 44
SLADE Frances dau of Edward and Ellen W. Slade, b Mar 1 1853, bapt Jun 24
1853 p 40
SLOTBY Maria Louisa (erratum: see also Hobby, Maria Louisa) m to William
Plater of St. Mary's County on Jul 22 1837; Miss Hobby was from Baltimore
p 108
SMITH Rev'd A.D. officiated at the wedding of Lewis H. Gibson of Zanesville
OH and Claribel B. Crumpton of Baltimore, on Dec 20 1893 at 4:00 p.m. at
E. Mt. Royal Avenue p 130
SMITH Ann m to David Hill of Philadelphia on Jun 28 1837; Miss Smith was
from Baltimore p 108

SMITH Anna Le Messurier dau of John Le Messurier and Sophia P. Smith, b Aug 1
   1838, bapt Sep 20 1838 p 23
SMITH Constant Freeman son of John Le Messurier and Sophia P. Smith, b Jan 23
   1835, bapt Jul 7 1836 p 21
SMITH Eliza bapt Feb 17 1851 p 37
SMITH Flora C. m to Edmond Byrne on Oct 5 1835, both of Baltimore p 107
SMITH John Le Messurier m to Sophia Price Freeman on Jun 27 1829, both of
   Baltimore, p of Constant Freeman p 21, Anna Le Messurier p 23, p 105
SMITH Miss Laura listed as a comm of the church in Sep 1869 p 82
SMITH Miss Rebecca listed as a comm of the church on Sep 1869 p 81
SMITH Rebecca and Laura, adults bapt on Apr 9 1850 p 35
SMITH Samuel bapt on Feb 15 1851 p 36
SOUTHWORTH George Pringle conf on May 31 1914 by Alfred Rodman Hussey p 93
SOWERS Eloza (see also Sowers, Eliza) m to Robert Steele on Oct 1 1839, both
   of Baltimore County p 108
SOWERS Prudence Ann m to Edward Taylor in 1840, both of Baltimore p 109
SPARKS Jared commenced the parish records of the First Independent Church of
   Baltimore, baptisms p 2, marriages p 101; officiated at the bapt of three
   children of John M. and Louisa Foster on May 19 1822 pp 2, 1, 101
SPARROW Clarinda m to Samuel E. Turner, bapt Jan 10 1847, b Dec 4 1824 p 32
STACEY Mary m to William Whitfield on Mar 25 1824, both of Baltimore p 103
STANLEY John m to Catherine A. Grammer on Feb 1 1855 p 115
STEARNS Charlotte Champe dau of Thomas and Mary Stearns, b Oct 23 1843, bapt
   Oct 13 1845 p 31
STEARNS Ellen Farley dau of Thomas and Mary Stearns, b Sep 29 1841, bapt
   Oct 13 1845 p 31
STEARNS George m to Fannie Merryman on Jun 28 1866 in Baltimore, John F.W.
   Ware officiating p 121
STEARNS Mrs. listed as a comm of the church in 1865 p 79
STEARNS Mrs. Mary listed as a comm of the church in Sep 1869 p 81
STEARNS Thomas and Mary p of Charlotte Champe p 31, Ellen Farley p 31
STEELE Anne m to William Robinson Jr. on May 4 1831, both of Baltimore p 106
STEELE Robert m to Eloza Sowers on Oct 1 1839, both of Baltimore County p 108
STEIGELMANN Jeannette m to Harry Man Rowe on Jan 6 1915 at 10:00 a.m. at
   Woodlawn, Baltimore County, Alfred Rodman Hussey officiating p 136
STERRETT Louisa R. m to Hamilton Potts on Jun 1 1844 p 110
STEUART Edith Hoyt dau of James M. and Sarah E. Steuart, b at Milford MA on
   Feb 8 1875, bapt on Apr 3 1896, Good Friday, conf on Apr 3 1896, Good
   Friday, joined the church on Apr 5 1896, Easter Sunday pp 70-1/2, 87
STEUART James M. and Sarah E. p of Edith Hoyt pp 70-1/2, 87
STEWARD Bertha Hoyt conf on Whitsunday Jun 11 1905, Alfred Rodman Hussey
   officiating p 91
STOCKHAUSEN Charles L. b Mar 10 1874, conf and joined the church on Nov 6 1892,
   m to Katharine Virginia Kesler on Sep 24 1903 at 8:00 p.m. in the church,
   both of Baltimore, Alfred Rodman Hussey officiating pp 86, 133
STONE Aaron Augustus son of Seth and Martha Stone, b Oct 28 1831, bapt Mar 4
   1832 p 17
STONE Seth and Martha p of Aaron Augustus p 17
STONESIFER Helen C. m to Harvey N. Wood on Nov 22 1915 at 1314 Bolton Street,
   both of Baltimore, Alfred Rodman Hussey officiating p 137
STRASSER Frederick b Aug 7 1873, conf and joined the church on Nov 6 1892
   p 36 (erratum), p 86

STRASSER Frederick Jr. m to Elsie E. Wolf on Jul 4 1897, Sunday, at 12:30
in the church; Mr. Strasser was from Baltimore p 132

STRASSER Maggie Virginia dau of ------Strasser, b Nov 24 1893, bapt May 13
1894 during Whitsunday service p 69

STREETER Caroline E. m to B. Franklin Beal on Oct 18 1855 p 115

STUART Anna Eastman dau of Guy Bryan and Anna Eastman Stuart, b Mar 31 1883,
bapt May 17 1891 p 65

STUART Edith May dau of Guy B. and Edith May (Eastman) Stuart, b Dec 6 1875,
bapt Jun 4 1876 p 54

STUART Guy B. m to Edith M. Eastman on Jan 12 1875, both of Baltimore, p of
Edith May pp 54, 125

STUART Guy Bryan and Anna Eastman Stuart p of Anna Eastman p 65

STUART Marie m to William Green on Aug 13 1857 p 116

STUART William m to Sue Campbell of Baltimore on Oct 1 1895 at 7:00 p.m. in
the church; Mr. Stuart was from Scotland p 131

STURGIS Russell m to Margaret Dawes Appleton on Dec 19 1835, p of Russell
pp 22, 107

STURGIS Russell son of Russell and Margaret D. Sturgis, b Oct 15 1836, bapt
Feb 23 1837 p 22

STURTEVANT F. Raymond Rev. entered the marriage of Paul E. Gesiger and Ella
Jautsch, both of Baltimore, on Jun 8 1925, who were married by Rev. Charles
G. Girelius at his residence p 138

STUTZ Walter F. m to Anna Coleell on Dec 30 1919, both of Washington DC,
Charles A. Wing officiating p 137

SULLIVAN Eleanor m to William I. Taylor on Apr 29 1918, both of Elmira NY
p 137

SUMNER Angeline W. b Jun 3 1834, d Jan 19 1920, buried Jan 21 1920, Rev. C.C.
Clark officiating (This funeral service took place after Charles A. Wing
resigned as minister and before his successor arrived.) p 97

SUMNER Emeline m to Charles Russell Pearce on Nov 11 1825 by William H. Furness
p 103

SUMNER Helen Payson dau of Henry P. and Fanny Sumner, b Feb 5 1836, bapt Jun 3
1836 p 21

SUMNER Henry P. and Fanny p of William Henry P 18, Helen Payson p 21, Rose
Allandale p 24

SUMNER Henry P. and Frances p of John Steel (see also John Hull) p 4

SUMNER John Steel (see also Sumner, John Hull) son of Henry and Frances Sumner,
b in Jul, bapt Oct 22, 1819 p 4

SUMNER Rose Allandale (Allhhby? Allenby?) dau of Henry P. and Fanny Sumner, b
May 7 1839, bapt Jun 18 1839 p 24

SUMNER Valeria dau of Henry P. and ------Sumner, bapt Jan 1 1824 p 12

SUMNER William Henry son of Henry P. and Fanny Sumner, b Jan 7 1834, bapt
May 31 1834 p 18

SWEET Caroline Mackintosh dau of Hartford and Isabella Sweet, b Aug 6 1850,
bapt Jun 3 1851 p 37

SWEET Hartford m to Isabella McDermot on Nov 6 1849, p of Caroline Mackintosh
p 37, Jacob Carman p 42, p 112

SWEET Jacob Carman son of Hartford and Isabella Sweet, b Aug 18 1852, bapt
May 13 1855 p 42

SWEETING Mary A. m to John Hastings on May 7 1822, both of Baltimore p 102

SWETT Moses of New York, m to Susan Ann Penniman of Baltimore on Sep 24 1833
p 107

TALIAFERRO Miss Byrd listed as a comm of the church in 1869 p 81
TALIAFERRO Miss listed as a member of the church in 1865 p 79
TAYLOR Edward m to Prudence Ann Sowers in 1840, both of Baltimore p 109
TAYLOR William I. m to Eleanor A. Sullivan on Apr 29 1918, both of Elmira NY
    p 137
THAYER Jennie Lucile m to Bruce K. Jerwald(?) on Oct 28 1914 at 12:00 noon
    at 1735 Linden Avenue; Miss Thayer was from Baltimore; Mr. Jerwald was
    from Philadelphia p 136
THAYER N. J. listed as a comm of the church in Sep 1869 p 82
THOMAS Frank son of Isaac Smith and Sarah Thomas, b Jul 1835, bapt Oct 25
    1835 p 20
THOMAS Isaac Smith son of Isaac Smith and Sarah Thomas, b Aug 31 1833, bapt
    Oct 25 1835 p 20
THOMAS (Thomans?) Isaac Smith and Sarah p of Thomas Sheppard p 20, Isaac
    Smith p 20, Frank p 20
THOMAS Thomas Sheppard son of Isaac Smith and Sarah Thomas, b Apr 12 1831,
    bapt Oct 25 1835 p 20
THOMPSON Mrs. J.F. listed as a comm of the church in 1865 p 78
THOMSEN Alonzo Lilly son of John J. and Emma Thomsen, b Sep 1 1855, bapt
    Oct 14 1856 p 44
THOMSEN John J. m to Emma Lilly on Oct 10 1854 p 114
THOMSEN John J. and Emma p of Alonzo Lilly p 44
TIFFANY Alfred son of Osmond and Ann Tiffany, b Oct 23 1852, bapt Jan 9 1853
    p 39
TIFFANY Ann Shaw dau of Osmond and Ann P. Tiffany, b Nov 21 1850, bapt Dec 29
    1850, m to Edward Bradley Jones on Jan 26 1881 at the church, both of
    Baltimore pp 36, 126
TIFFANY Anne Checkley dau of Osmond and Ann Tiffany, bapt Jul 1 1832, listed
    as a comm of the church in Sep 1869 pp 17, 81
TIFFANY Mrs. Anne P. listed as a comm of the church in Sep 1869 p 81
TIFFANY Beatrice conf during the ministry of C.R. Weld 1877, m to Francis S.
    Key Jun 29 1889 at 10:00 a.m. in the church, both of Baltimore pp 85, 128
TIFFANY Charlotte dau of Osmond and Ann Tiffany, b Mar 23 1833, bapt Apr 14
    1833 p 17
TIFFANY Edward son of O. C. and Ann Tiffany, bapt Mar 15 1830 p 15
TIFFANY Francis m to Esther A. Brown on Oct 14 1852 p 114
TIFFANY George Peabody son of George Peabody Tiffany and Anne Dickey Tiffany,
    b Jan 22 1859, bapt May 21 1859 p 47
TIFFANY George Peabody son of Osmond Tiffany and Wife, bapt Jan 11 1829,
    father of George Peabody p 47, listed as a comm of the church in 1865 and
    in 1869 pp 15, 47, 78, 81
TIFFANY Osmond son of Osmond C(apron) and Ann Checkley Shaw, bapt Sep 23 1823,
    m to Ann Pinkney White on Oct 5 1847, p of Ann Shaw p 36, Alfred p 39,
    pp 10, 112
TIFFANY Osmond C(apron) and Ann Checkley Shaw p of Osmond p 10, George Peabody
    p 15, Edward p 15, Ann Checkley p 17, Charlotte p 17
TIFFANY Osmond Checkley son of William C. and Elizabeth Howard Tiffany, b
    Nov 26 1857, bapt Mar 23 1858 p 47
TIFFANY William C. and Elizabeth Howard p of Osmond Checkley p 45
TILISTON Martha Elizabeth dau of William and Martha Tiliston, b Mar 9 1833,
    bapt Oct 1 1841 p 26
TILISTON Sarah Appleton dau of William and Martha Tiliston, b Dec 7 1834,
    bapt Oct 1 1841 p 26

TILISTON William and Martha (Marston) p of Martha Elizabeth p 26, Sarah Appleton p 26, m on Oct 11 1832, both of Baltimore pp 26, 106

TORSCH Althea Louisa (see also Torch) dau of C. Burnett and Mathilde (Praeger) Torsch, bapt at the home of her parents in Catonsville MD on Jun 22 1905 during the ministry of Alfred Rodman Hussey p 72

TORSCH C. Burnett and Mathilde (Praeger) (see also Torch) p of Althea Louise p 72

TORSCH Henry F. (see also Torch) joined the church on Easter Sunday 1900 p 89

TROW Orin C. m to Nina R. Petri on Jun 8 1858 p 117

TROWBRIDGE -? listed as a comm of the church in 1865 p 78

TROWBRIDGE James son of James Trowbridge and wife, bapt Jul 12 1831 p 16

TROWBRIDGE Reuben listed as a comm of the church in Sep 1869 p 81

TUFTS William m to Mrs. Rebecca Frieze on Sep 13 1832, both of Baltimore p 106

TURNER Clarinda Sparrow wife of Samuel E. Turner, bapt Jan 10 1847, b Dec 4 1824 p 32

TURNER J. E. listed as a comm of the church in 1865 p 78

TURNER Samuel E. son of Samuel E. Turner and Clarinda Sparrow Turner, b Sep 6 1846, bapt Jan 10 1847 p 32

TURNER Samuel E. and Clarinda Sparrow Turner p of Samuel E. Turner p 32

TWAMLEY Susie Belle m to Frederick W. Werner of Baltimore on May 4 1892 at 7:30 p.m. in the Chapel of the church; Miss Twamley was from Troy p 130

UTHMAN John T. m to Martha G. Osborne on Nov 16 1854 p 115

VALENTINE Richard G. and Ann p of Margaret Colt, b Jul 31 1831, John b Dec 2 1833, both children bapt on Sep 27 1836 p 21

VAN HOOF Maria T.M. of Antwerp, Belgium, m to Rena Mennen of Baltimore on Oct 29 1921 in the church, Harry Foster Burns officiating p 138

VAUGHEN Miss Rachel listed as a comm of the church in Sep 1869 p 82

VEDDER Charles A. m to Sophia S. Gray on May 5 1908 at 10:30 a.m. at 1314 Bolton Street, both of Baltimore, Alfred R. Hussey officiating p 134

VOCKE Emma Elizabeth (Simon) m to George H. Vocke on Nov 4 1886 in the church at 1:30 p.m., p of Stanley Torney, b Aug 8 1887, bapt Dec 25 1887 in Baltimore County pp 63,127

VROOMAN Walter m to Anne L. Grafflin of Baltimore on Feb 25 1897 at 10:00 a.m. Thursday at 1123 St. Paul Street p 132

WADSWORTH Alice Mowe b Oct 3 1845 in Eastport ME, bapt May 29 1887, Whitsunday, in church p 62

WADSWORTH Herbert and Alice Mowe Wadsworth p of Robert Mowe p 62

WADSWORTH Robert Mowe son of Herbert and Alice Mowe Wadsworth, b Aug 17 1875 in Battleboro VT, bapt May 29 1887, Whitsunday, in church p 62

WAINWRIGHT Charles Dexter son of Henry E. and Sarah B. Wainwright, b Apr 17 1856, bapt on Oct 26 1856 in Boston p 44

WAINWRIGHT Henry E. and Sarah B. p of Charles Dexter p 44

WALDKOENIG Emma conf and joined the church on May 21 1893, Whitsunday, b Dec 8 1876 p 87

WALDSCHMIDT Albert conf Easter Sunday 1900 p 88

WALDSCHMIDT Charles conf and joined the church on Nov 6 1892, b Jan 30 1874 p 86

WALKER Franklin son of John and ------Walker, bapt May 6 1838 p 23

WALKER John and Wife p of Franklin Walker p 23

WALKINSHAW Robert B. (see also Walkinstraw, Robert B.(?)) of Tacoma WA, m to Jeanie M. Walter of Baltimore on Jun 10 1914 at 6:30 p.m. at 2801 North Charles Street p 136

WALKLEY Albert officiated at the wedding of Carl George Hilgenberg and
   Angelica Ragge on Jan 11 1898 at 6:00 p.m. (Tuesday), in the church,
   both of Baltimore p 132
WALLENSTEIN Fannie a Jewess, of Baltimore, m to William M. Keighler of New
   York City on Apr 23 1878 p 126
WALSH Helen of Philadelphia PA m to Ira John Perry of St. Louis MO on Nov 19
   1914 at 1:15 p.m. at 221 W. Center Street, Alfred Rodman Hussey officiating
   p 136
WALTER Jeanie M. of Baltimore, m to Robert B. Walkinshaw of Tacoma WA on Jun
   10 1914 at 6:30 p.m. at 2801 North Charles Street, Alfred Rodman Hussey
   officiating p 136
WALWORTH Edna A. of Baltimore m to William Herbert Gorsuch of Baltimore
   County on Dec 11 1894 at 7:00 p.m. in church p 131
WALWORTH H.R. listed as a comm of the church in Sep 1869 p 82
WARD Benjamin C. and Eliza p of Julia Elizabeth Ward p 17
WARD Elizabeth S. m to Thomas W. Hall on May 22 1832, both of Baltimore p 106
WARD Julia Elizabeth dau of Benjamin C. and Eliza Ward, b Dec 19 1831, bapt
   Apr 8 1832 p 17
WARE John F.W., Marriages performed by: Cephas Dodd McFarland and Emily W.
   Chubb 1865, Edwin Mimfield(?) and Sarah E. Coy 1866, George Stearns and
   Fannie Merryman 1866, William Henry Keith and Clemence T. Hyde 1866, George
   F. Granniss and Matilda J. Burgess 1866, Richard K. Perkins and Amanda M.
   Pierce 1866, James A. Miller and Eva R. Martin 1866, Sherman Conant and
   Frances Dewry 1867, William Lea Jr. and Sarah B. Bentky 1867 pp 121, 122
WARE Preston Jr. m to Lavinia Lilly on Jun 16 1846 p 111
WARRINGTON Elmer James son of Joseph A. and Lillie Warrington, b Apr 24 1895,
   bapt Nov 10 1895 in church p 70
WARRINGTON Joseph A. and Lillie p of Elmer James p 70
WATKINS Decimus Eugene son of Tobias and ------Watkins, b in Baltimore, bapt
   Oct 10 1819 p 4
WATKINS Tobias and Wife p of Decimus Eugene p 4
WATSON Alverta Patten Cecinghey(?) dau of John and Mary Watson, b Aug 1844,
   bapt Oct 7 1844 p 30
WATSON Charlotte Beauregard dau of ------Watson, bapt 1866 p 48
WATSON James George son of John and Mary Watson, b Jan 8 1853, bapt Feb 18
   1853 p 39
WATSON John and Mary p of Alverta p 30, Prudence Osborn p 32, James George
   p 39
WATSON Margaret dau of Thomas C. and Mary Watson, b Oct 13 1854, bapt Jan 3
   1855 p 41
WATSON Mary Jane dau of Thomas C. and Mary Watson, b Nov 18 1856, bapt Dec 9
   1856 p 44
WATSON Prudence Osborn dau of John and Mary Watson, b Jul 19 1847 (erratum:
   b 1839, see Maryland Census, Baltimore City, 1850, p 301, 3 ward) bapt
   Apr 27 1847 p 32
WATSON Samuel Ferguson son of Thomas C. and Mary Watson, b Dec 13 1849, bapt
   Apr 3 1850 p 35
WATSON Sarah m to George Forbes on Oct 31 1850 p 113
WATSON Sarah Ann m to Alfred Schucking on Jun 6 1846 p 111
WATSON Thomas C. and Mary p of Samuel Ferguson p 35, Margaret p 41, Mary Jane
   p 44
WAXTER Elizabeth conf during the ministry of Charles Richmond Weld on Jun 8
   1878 p 85

WAXTER Emma Tracy conf during the ministry of Charles Richmond Weld on Jun 8
    1878 p 85
WEBSTER John Lee bapt on Apr 17 1854, adult p 41
WEEDON Margaret E. of Baltimore, m to Alexander E. Bauhan of Holtwood PA on
    Feb 2 1918 p 137
WELD C.K. (erratum: see Weld, C.R.), Marriages during the ministry of ------
    p 125
WELD Charles Richmond, Baptisms during the ministry of ------ p 52,
    Confirmations during the ministry of ------ p 85
WELD Eliza Gould dau of George F. Weld and Wife, b Jan 16 1834, bapt Dec 25
    1839 p 24
WELD Francis (see also George Francis p 24)
WELD Franklin son of George F. and Sarah (?) Weld, b Apr 18 1841, bapt Dec 25
    1841 p 26
WELD George son of George F. and Sarah Weld, b Sep 3 1844, bapt Feb 2 1847 p 32
WELD George F. and Sarah p of Sarah Abby, James Gould, Elizabeth Gould,
    Rebecca, George Francis, Franklin, George pp 24, 26, 32
WELD George Francis son of George F. Weld and Wife, b Jul 11 1839, bapt Dec 25
    1839 p 24
WELD James Gould son of George F. Weld and Wife, b Feb 24 1832, bapt Dec 25
    1839 p 24
WELD Rebecca dau of George F. Weld and Wife, b May 25 1836, bapt Dec 25 1839
    p 24
WELD Sarah Abby dau of George F. Weld and Wife, b Jul 8 1829, bapt Dec 25 1839
    p 24
WELKE Charles Louis m to Mary Louise Rixse on Sep 25 1898 by Reverend William
    H. Cole of Cohasset MA, conf on Easter Sunday 1900 p 132, 88
WELKE Charles Louis and Mary Louise p of Melvin Louis Welke p 71
WELKE Melvin Louis son of Charles Louis and Mary Louise Welke, b Sep 24 1899,
    bapt on Sunday Oct 29 1899 by Rev. William B. Geoghegan of Berkeley CA p 71
WENTZ Sarah C. conf on Whitsunday May 19 1907 by Alfred Rodman Hussey p 91
WERNER Charles Weld son of Frederick M. and Susie Belle (Twarnley?) Werner,
    b Nov 28 1893, bapt Mar 25, Easter Sunday, 1894 p 68
WERNER Frederick W. of Baltimore, m to Susie Belle Twarnley (Twamley?) of Troy
    on May 4 1892 at 7:30 p.m. in church, p of Henry Irving p 66, Charles Weld
    p 68, p 130
WERNER Henry Irving son of Frederick William and Susie Belle (Twarnley) Werner,
    b Sep 28 1892, bapt during Whitsunday service May 21 1893 in the chapel p 66
WEST Adeline m to Charles M. Jackson on Nov 22 1843 p 110
WEYRICH Anne dau of Jessie May (Stallings) Weyrich and Harry Stansbury Weyrich,
    b Jun 4 1919, bapt Nov 23 1919 in church, Charles A. Wing officiating p 75
WEYRICH Harry Stansbury and Jessie May (Stallings) Weyrich p of Anne p 75,
    Harry Stansbury Weyrich was conf on Easter Sunday Apr 7 1912 by Alfred
    Rodman Hussey pp 75, 93
WEYRICH Joseph Lewis b Sep 21 1889, d Oct 8 1918, memorial service in the
    church on Oct 11 1918, Charles A. Wing officiating p 95
WHITE Annie P. (see also White, Anne P.) m to Osmond Tiffany on Oct 5 1847 p 112
WHITE Campbell Pinkney son of Joseph and Isabella White, bapt May 11 1841 p 25
WHITE Cornelia Emily dau of Joseph and Isabella White, bapt May 11 1841 p 25
WHITE Edward Campbell son of John and Mary White, b Apr 13 1841, bapt May 11
    1841 p 25
WHITE Isabel dau of Joseph and Isabella White, bapt Mar 5 1823 p 10
WHITE Isabella (Mrs.) listed as a comm of the church in Sep 1869 p 81

WHITE James and Isabella p of Mary p 70-1/2, Margaret Elizabeth p 71
WHITE John and Mary p of Edward Campbell p 25, William Campbell p 27, Joseph
    p 29
WHITE Joseph son of John and Mary White, b Sep 21 1843, bapt Mar 6 1844 p 29
WHITE Joseph and Isabella p of Isabel p 10, William Pickney p 25, Cornelia
    Emily p 25, Campbell Pickney p 25
WHITE Margaret Elizabeth dau of James White and Isabella White, b Nov 16
    1896, bapt Oct 24 1897 p 71
WHITE Mary dau of James and Isabella White, b Apr 18 1895 at 114 E. Monument
    Street in Baltimore, bapt Feb 2 1896 p 70-1/2
WHITE William Campbell son of John C. and Mary White, b May 26 1842, bapt
    Dec 18 1842 p 27
WHITE William Pickney son of Joseph and Isabella White, bapt May 11 1841 p 25
WHITELOCK George b Dec 25 1854, d Jan 8 1920, funeral Jan 10 1920, Rev. Frank
    C. Doan officiating p 97
WHITFIELD William m to Miss Mary Stacey on Mar 25 1824, both of Baltimore p 103
WHITING Rose M. (see also Whitney, Rose M.) m to Thomas A.E. Moreley on May 22
    1913 at 8 p.m. in the church, Alfred Rodman Hussey officiating p 136
WHITTIER Augusta A. m to George F. Emerson on Apr 21 1851 p 113
WILBUR William H. m to Ida B. Lucke, both of Baltimore, on Jun 10 1911 at 3 p.m.
    at 3605 Windsor Mill Road, Walbrook, Alfred Rodman Hussey officiating p 135
WILKENS William B. m to Sarah E. Houston on Nov 25 1855 p 115
WILLARD Henry Kellogg conf on Oct 29 1887 during the ministry of Charles
    Richmond Weld, b Oct 20 1856 in Washington DC p 86
WILLIAMS Caroline Helen dau of Nathl. and Caroline Williams, bapt on Feb 21
    1822, m to William Remington on Feb 10 1846 pp 7, 111
WILLIAMS Cumberland D. and Betsey p of Edward p 3
WILLIAMS Edward son of Cumberland D. and Betsey Williams, bapt Jul 10 1819 p 3
WILLIAMS Edward P. and Frances R. p of Emily p 28
WILLIAMS Elizabeth Dorsey dau of John H. and Annie Williams, bapt May 17 1874,
    at 14 McCullough Street p 53
WILLIAMS Emily dau of Edward P. and Frances Rebecca, b Feb 8 1843, bapt May
    21 1843 p 28
WILLIAMS Emily Louisa m to Bethune Washburn Hewson of Petersburg on Nov 2
    1830 p 105
WILLIAMS H. H., Susan Campbell Williams was bapt at his home on Nov 27 1869
    p 50
WILLIAMS Henry H. and Rebecca p of John Howell p 19, Samuel St. John p 19,
    James Wright p 22
WILLIAMS James Wright son of Henry H. and Rebecca Williams, b Aug 9 1837,
    bapt Dec 25 1837 p 22
WILLIAMS John B. and Sarah F. p of Piercy Garnet p 45
WILLIAMS John Bullard son of John J. Williams of Glyndon MD, b Oct 4 1875,
    bapt Jun 9 1889, Whitsunday, in church p 63
WILLIAMS John H. and Annie C. p of Susan Campbell p 50, Elizabeth Dorsey p 53,
    John Howell p 53
WILLIAMS John Howell son of Henry H. and Rebecca Williams, b Dec 14 1832,
    bapt Jun 18 1835 p 19
WILLIAMS John Howell son of John H. and Annie Williams, bapt May 17 1874 at
    14 McCullough Street p 53
WILLIAMS John J. father of John Bullard p 63
WILLIAMS Joshua Barney son of Nathaniel and Caroline Williams, bapt Sep 17
    1819 p 4

WILLIAMS Martha E. m to Nathaniel F. Williams on Jul 3 1845 p 110
WILLIAMS Nancy Clark m to Mr. John Leverett Moore of Orange NJ on Dec 23 1891
   at 915 McCulloh Street at 7:30 p.m., Miss Williams was from Baltimore p 123
WILLIAMS Nathaniel and Caroline p of Joshua Barney p 4, Caroline Helen p 7
WILLIAMS Nathaniel F. m to Martha E. Williams on Sep 3 1845, father of
   Nathaniel Felton pp 33, 110
WILLIAMS Nathaniel Felton son of Nathaniel F. and Martha E. Williams, b Jun 3
   1847, bapt Jul 3 1847 p 33
WILLIAMS Piercy Garnet son of John B. and Sarah F. Williams, b May 4 1857, bapt
   Sep 18 1857 p 45
WILLIAMS Samuel H. (erratum: see Williams, Samuel St. John p 19)
WILLIAMS Sarah E. m to George W. Miltenberger on May 2 1850 p 112
WILLIAMS Susan Campbell dau of John H. and Annie C. Williams, bapt during the
   ministry of E.C. Guild on Nov 27 1869 at the house of Mr. H.H. Williams, m
   to William Stuart of Scotland on Oct 1 1895 at 7:00 in the evening in the
   church pp 50, 131
WILLIAMS Theodore bapt Margaret Elizabeth, dau of William H. and Margaret
   Green Shelton, b Jan 14 1899, on Apr 2 1899 in church p 71
WILLIAMS Miss Victoria listed as a comm of the church in Sep 1869 p 81
WILSON Adelheid Magdalene dau of Andrew H. and Margaret Elizabeth (Herges)
   Wilson, b Apr 25 1885, bapt during Whitsunday service in the chapel on
   May 21 1893 p 66
WILSON Andrew H. and Margaret Elizabeth (Herges) Wilson, p of Adelheid
   Magdalene p 66, Mabel Cora p 66
WILSON Mabel Cora dau of Andrew H. and Mabel Cora (Herges) Wilson, b Feb 5
   1859, bapt May 21 1893 p 66
WING Rev. Charles A., Baptisms during the ministry of p 75, Funerals during
   the ministry of pp 95, 97, Marriages during the ministry of p 137
WINSEY Herbert conf on Easter Sunday Apr 14 1895 p 87
WISTER Charles Kemble Butler son of Owen Wister and the late Mary (Channing)
   Wister, bapt Jan 17 1914 at 1112 Spence Street, Philadelphia p 74
WISTER Owen and Mary (Channing) Wister p of Charles Kemble Butler p 74,
   Sarah Butler p 74
WISTER Sarah Butler dau of Owen Wister and the late Mary (Channing) Wister,
   b Aug 1913, bapt Jan 17 1914 at 1112 Spence Street, Philadelphia p 74
WISWALL Edmund F. m to Sophia M. Baird on Dec 4 1856 p 116
WOLF Elsie E. m to Frederick Strasser of Baltimore on Jul 4 1897 at 12:30
   in church, a Sunday p 132
WOLLINGTON James E. m to Frances J. Kilbourn on Oct 24 1854 p 115
WOOD Caroline conf on Easter Sunday Apr 16 1911, Alfred Rodman Hussey
   officiating, m to Harrison Bliss of Providence RI Aug 31 1918, Charles A.
   Wing officiating p 137
WOOD Dorothy conf on Whitsunday May 19 1907, Alfred Rodman Hussey officiating
   p 91
WOOD Elizabeth conf on Whitsunday May 20 1909, Alfred Rodman Hussey
   officiating, m to Clarke F. Freeman of Providence RI on Feb 1 1919 (Miss
   Wood was from Baltimore), Charles A. Wing officiating pp 92, 137
WOOD Elizabeth Ann dau of Harvey N. Wood and Helen (Stonesifer) Wood, b Jan
   29 1917, bapt Jun 5 1921 in church p 76
WOOD Harvey N. m to Helen C. Stonesifer on Nov 22 1915 at 1314 Bolton Street,
   Alfred Rodman Hussey officiating, both of Baltimore p 137
WOOD Helen conf on Easter Sunday Apr 16 1911, Alfred Rodman Hussey officiating
   p 92

WOOD Helen Catherine Stonesifer and Harvey N. Wood p of John Robert p 76, Jay
    Harvey p 76, Elizabeth Ann p 76
WOOD Jay Harvey son of Helen Catherine (Stonesifer) Wood and Harvey N. Wood,
    b Feb 10 1920, bapt Jun 5 1921 p 76
WOOD John Robert son of Helen Catherine (Stonesifer) Wood and Harvey N. Wood,
    b Dec 31 1912, bapt Jun 5 1921 p 76
WORCH Marie Edwina conf and joined the church on Whitsunday Jun 6 1897 p 88
WRENN Harold H. m to Elizabeth Jencks on Nov 29 1919, the former from Norfolk
    VA, the latter of Baltimore p 137
WRIGHT John W. m to Abbie E. Cunningham on Jun 1856 p 116
WYETH Charles m to Caroline K. Bartlett on Jul 16 1859 p 117
WYETH Elizabeth Jarvis dau of Leonard J. and Caroline Wyeth, bapt on Mar 9
    1823 p 10
WYETH Leonard J. m to Miss Caroline Archer on Oct 2 1821, both of Baltimore
    p 102
WYETH Leonard J. and Caroline p of Elizabeth Jarvis p 10
YAEGER Charles Bradford son of Louis and Emma Augusta (Jones) Yaeger, b Oct 8
    1893, bapt Mar 25 1894, Easter Sunday, in church p 68
YAEGER Louis and Emma Augusta (Jones) p of Charles Bradford p 68
YOUNG Alexander m to Ann Maria Raub on Jul 20 1847 p 111
YOUNG Alexander and Anna M. p of Ida p 39, Kate p 39
YOUNG Ida dau of Alexander and Anna M. Young, b Nov 9 1849, bapt Apr 5 1853
    p 39
YOUNG Kate dau of Alexander and Anna M. Young, b Feb 19 1852, bapt Apr 5 1853
    p 39
YOUNG Louis F. b 1850, d Jun 6 1920, funeral 9 1920, Rev. C.C. Clark
    officiating p 97
YOUNG Louis F. m to Frankie E. Boughman on May 6 1875 at the church at 10:00
    a.m., both of Baltimore p 125
ZENKER (Zenkes?) David m to Kate Kuhn of Baltimore on Nov 3 1886 in the church
    at 7:00 p.m. (David was from Kent County MD) p 127
ZENKER (Zenkes?) James David and Mary Catharine (Kuhn) Zenker (Zenkes?) p of
    Laura Elizabeth p 69
ZENKER (Zenkes?) Laura Elizabeth dau of James David and Mary Catharine
    Zenker (Zenkes?), b at Catonsville May 15 1894, bapt Dec 9 1894 p 69
ZENKES (Zenker?) Charles Wilbur son of James David Zenkes (Zenker?) and
    Katharine (Kuhn) Zenkes (Zenker?) b in Kent County MD on Oct 18 1887, bapt
    in church on Sunday Nov 27 1887 p 63
ZENKES (Zenker?) James David and Katharine (Kuhn) p of Charles Wilbur p 68
ZWISSLER Eleanora conf and joined the church on Apr 14, Palm Sunday, 1889
    p 86

9 781585 495078